Compliance to Commercial

The **QUIET** approach to Finance Business Partnering

ANDREW JEPSON

Compliance to Commercial
The QUIET approach to Finance Business Partnering

First published in Australia by Vincero Consulting 2018
www.vinceroconsulting.com.au

Prepublication Data Service details available from
The National Library of Australia
ISBN: 978-0-6483423-0-4 (pbk)
ISBN: 978-0-6483423-1-1 (ebk)

Typesetting and design by Publicious Book Publishing
Published in collaboration with Publicious Book Publishing
www.publicious.com.au

Dedicated to Kimberley, surround yourself with people who support and inspire you.

Contents

Foreword

Finance Business Partnering has become a buzz topic in the accounting and finance industry recently. Why? I'm not sure. The reality is the concept and the best accountants have been doing this for decades. The best accountants have been adding value for many years and have become key people within their respective organisations. They are highly valued and are often afforded more lucrative career opportunities, along with the chance to work on the business critical issues within an organisation or business unit.

Whether we classify them as finance business partners, commercial managers, management accountants or whatever other title we can bestow upon them, one thing is common to these people. They do more than transactional finance. They do more than interpret complex accounting rules and regulations and tell us which line of the P&L and balance sheet to put them. They do more than reporting. They do more than the laborious tasks of compliance. These accountants embed themselves in a business, spend time understanding how it works and then work with the other functions to bring value to the organisation.

I spent ten years of my accounting career performing the compliance-type work. Audits, statutory reports, controls and governance. But I wasn't satisfied. I wanted to work "in" the organisation that had employed me.

I wanted to make them more money or save them more money. I wanted to help them reach their strategic objectives or at the very least help management achieve their KPIs.

So, I spent the next ten years of my career doing that. And this is where the job satisfaction, engagement, empowerment and enjoyment in my career began to be fulfilled.

During this time, I led large teams of commercial accountants as well as working as part of the Chartered Accountants of Australia and New Zealand, facilitating and marking exams for the technical modules of the CA Program. I secretly enjoyed this as it gave me a chance to be at the forefront of the knowledge newly qualified CAs had when they were completing their qualification (and I got paid for keeping my CPD hours up). What I found was that although most of these candidates and the staff who worked for me had a strong grasp of the technical knowledge in accounting and finance, they lacked the depth and breadth of that knowledge and being able to apply it commercially. And we were giving them 15 out of 20 in their mark sheets. And then putting the letter "C" and "A" after their name and sending them out into the world to advise on complex business issues. Should clients be paying for this without the required practical skills to apply that knowledge or the behavioural skills to communicate effectively with non-finance individuals?

The answer I kept coming back to was no.

Our professional bodies do a fantastic job of providing the technical knowledge and basis for a rewarding career in finance and accounting. But there is more to it if you want to be considered valuable in an organisation and help them make more money or save more money, reach their strategic objectives and achieve their KPIs. This niche of the finance and accounting industry is what other functions expect of us to add value.

So, I decided I wanted to do something about it. With our industry sitting in the perfect place to be automated by robotics and Artificial Intelligence, our ability to interpret information and add value is all we will have left once the machines roll in (its already happening with tasks being outsourced to people who know nothing about our organisations or even worse don't even have a name or a face).

But where do we begin when we are talking about a concept of Finance Business Partnership? A concept so broad and wide the material on it seems endless. A google search on the topic would lead you in several directions with several self-professed experts weighing in on the topic. Unfortunately, with all of this material there is no guiding framework out there that could help bring all of it under topics and buckets to help make sense of it all.

A framework is sadly missing – if only we had one it might make things a little easier. This book provides that framework.

In performing the research for this book, the other issue we discovered was that all of the material out there was being written from a finance perspective. It was being written by finance people about finance topics. And it was being written about topics and subjects that, frankly, most accountants and finance people already know about or have been trained in. Anybody who is working in an organisation is working in these topics all of the time – why would we want to read about them again. It was like a whole lot of high and mighty finance "experts" decided they would start writing about things that frustrated them, on topics they thought nobody else had worked out a solution to yet. It is the equivalent of telling someone it is their birthday – Is it really?

What was sadly lacking was – what do non-finance people want from finance?

Nobody in a non-finance function was busily writing blogs and articles about finance business partnering. I have yet to find an article written by a sales or marketing individual discussing the merits of finance business partnering. If we are to "partner" other functions effectively, wouldn't it be wise to research, listen to the other functions, and find out what they want from finance? We know what we want, there is plenty of material on that. If we can marry that up with what other functions want, we may be onto something that adds some real value to our organisations.

This book delivers on that.

It provides a framework to help you focus your efforts and diagnose problem areas in your finance business partnering journey. Taken out of research, and from the perspective of a non-finance individual.

I hope you enjoy the read. I firmly believe the accounting industry has the ability to offer some significant skills that robots cannot replicate. If we can develop these skills and behaviours we can start to add real value in the organisations we work, move our image from "Compliance to Commercial" and become not just accountants but real finance business partners.

Section A

The problem, the solution

The Accountant's Paradigm

Sitting in front of you are two accountants at very different stages of their careers and with different ideas about what success looks like.

Peter is a senior finance executive in his late 30s. He has had a varied career that started out of university working at a large multinational investment bank. He worked his way through three organisations in various analytical and business development roles and is now the Head of Commercial Finance for a large multinational with a team of six reporting into him. Peter is not a qualified accountant and does not have an accounting degree. His technical knowledge is considered limited as he does not know a lot about debits and credits, accounting standards or tax laws. What he does excel at is translating financial and numerical information into tangible business insight. He has partnered many different functions over his career including sales, marketing, supply chain and operations and worked on several IT and system related projects. He is currently being succession planned into the CFO role within the multinational organisation he works in.

Jessica is an ambitious young accountant. She has spent the last five or six years of her life dedicated to the accounting profession. After breezing through university with high marks, she started working in one of the Big Four accounting firms as an auditor. It is here she started her CA qualification and over the next two years managed to get through the rigours of one of the world's best post graduate study programs and achieved a merit mark in two of the five modules.

Following four to five years as an auditor working on some of the biggest clients in the country, she took the leap out of professional services and moved into a senior management accounting role in a large ASX company.

She is considered to be as technically strong as her peers in the field of accounting but is struggling to create influence in her organisation and is wondering what skills she is lacking that will help take her career to the next level. She has recently started her MBA as she sees this as a way of developing her skillset further in the finance and accounting field. She looks at the career of Peter and aspires to have a similar position in a few years' time.

What is Jessica doing that is not allowing her to progress to the level Peter is at? How has Peter managed to get so far in an accounting and finance career without having any technical accounting skills?

This is the Accountant's Paradigm.

And the Accountant's Paradigm needs to be understood if as an accountant you want to become a great finance business partner. Being a great accountant requires very different skills and behaviours to being a great finance business partner. And it is counterintuitive to everything we are taught as accountants when we are doing our professional training.

For Jessica the good news is that right now she is the smartest she will ever be. Right now, at this moment in her career, she is as technically smart as she will ever be in the accounting field. Jessica has just spent around two years studying everything, and she will never know more about technical accounting than she does now.

For Peter, unfortunately he is a long way past the smartest he will ever be. The last piece of formal technical training he did was in his commerce degree at university, plus some varied leadership training in the organisations he has been in.

But that is ok, because Peter has several other skills which put him comfortably in the position he is in as a Head of Commercial Finance of a large multinational. Peter has spent the last 10–15 years applying his financial and commercial acumen, his leadership skills and behaviours. And he has most likely spent a significant portion of his career doing this with non-finance professionals.

This is the Accountant's Paradigm.

Finance staff at early stages in their career believe their technical expertise is what will make them successful. And it most likely does; in an expert area such as tax or professional services (working in a Big Four firm or consulting). However, in a commercial organisation surrounded by non-finance people and complex variables, it is not what defines success.

This is The Accountant's Paradigm – how do I change everything

I have been taught and been conditioned to think like, in order to be successful in a role that requires a subtle change in skills, behaviours and approach?

Technical Knowledge

Let's demonstrate via a couple of diagrams (see Figure 1).

We will start with time across the bottom and level of competence up the side. The graphed line is your level of technical knowledge in accounting and finance. This line goes on an upward curve as you study for your professional qualification and peaks at the conclusion of that. Then you qualify, and slowly but surely this level of competence and knowledge decreases and flattens out. To a point where you now do not know as much from a technical standpoint as you used to. You haven't forgotten it, it's just become a little vague.

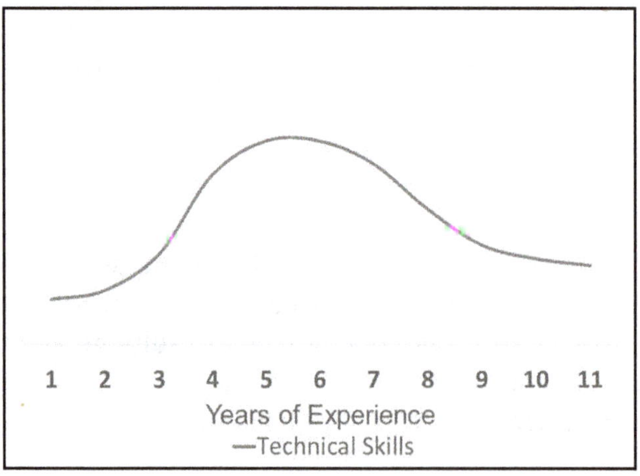

Figure 1: Technical knowledge

This is normal and nothing to be afraid of. The reason this happens is that a significant portion of the technical material you study in your qualification is often not used once you are in an organisation. This is especially true in a large organisation which is where a lot of staff out of Big Four firms first go, as there are several people focused on each specific area. Put another way, there are a number of subject matter experts in the organisation and you will be one of them for only a small portion of what you had previously studied.

I experienced this when I worked within a large ASX-listed multinational property company. My role was heavily focused on Financial Instruments, hedging and Shareplans. These are the accounting standards I spent all my time reading about and reviewing and I was an expert on them. I could even quote paragraphs of these standards. But if you asked me about them now I would have no idea, because I don't work with them any longer and truth be told, I couldn't care about them, as they don't help me make the organisations I work in more money/cash.

There must be something else going on, otherwise we would all finish our professional qualification and be at the top of our games. If having strong technical knowledge was what career success looks like for a finance business partner, Jessica would be in the best position in her career right now, and we all know that isn't what happens. If it was, Jessica would be the Head of Commercial Finance and Peter would be a junior staff member.

Remember Peter is considered to be one of the best finance business partners in the country and he isn't even a qualified accountant.

This is the Accountant's Paradigm.

So how do we break this paradigm? Our industry is heavily focused on training and conditioning us to be technical experts in our field. However, this knowledge and expertise is simply a hygiene factor when working in a commercial organisation. It is a ticket to the game. And sometimes it isn't even a ticket to the game as other business functions like sales, marketing, operations have little to no idea what you are talking about when you quote S6 of the Tax Act or IFRS 16.

So, what is going on here and how do we break this paradigm so we can move from technical experts to strong finance business partners?

There are two additional dynamics that define your success

Credibility

The first is your ability to apply those technical skills. Or your practical experience in applying them. Your business acumen, your analysis skills. I like to call this your "Organisational Acumen" and this is what helps you build your credibility in an organisation.

Done well people will want to work with you. And once you have that (credibility) only then can you start to influence them.

It looks like this:

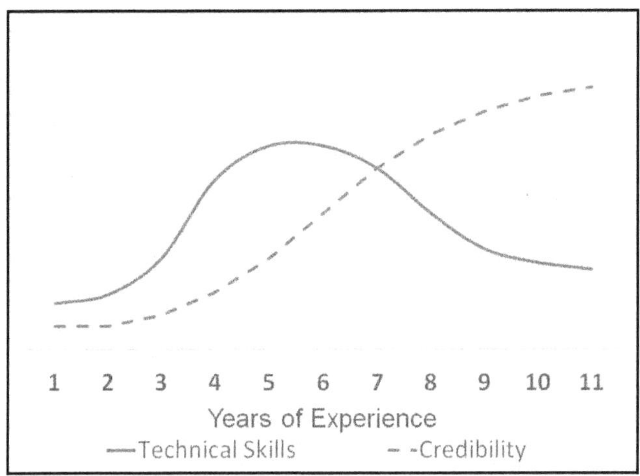

Figure 2: Credibility curve

This starts slowly as you learn to do tasks and things that you need to do to do your job in an organisation. You effectively just learn the normal things of what to do, usually via scripts, processes, etc.; anything you can document and instruct.

This then builds as you encounter ad-hoc pieces of work (projects), one-off issues, unusual problems and things that have not yet been encountered before by yourself or, more often than not, the rest of the finance team in the organisation.

This is your credibility curve.

This is where you take your technical skills and start to apply them to solving business problems, to resolve issues and to add value. And this can take some time, as you will need to learn how the organisation's business model works – where are the problems, what ideas do you have to tackle these issues and resolve?

This plays out like this. When I did tax in my professional qualification studies, I didn't work in tax and accordingly studied hard to ensure I didn't fail. What this led to was me receiving the highest mark in the firm I was in, in the tax module. If we asked the Institute who was the best person to look after a tax problem in the firm for staff at my level, those results would indicate me.

But I couldn't do a tax return, or tax planning, or solve a tax problem. As a tax problem solver, I was next to useless. I hadn't spent any time working on these issues for clients or attempting to apply my technical knowledge. I had no credibility.

Another example is of someone who I recently coached who was technically very strong. She had been promoted and I was brought in to ensure she continued to succeed in the organisation as identified talent. Four months after her promotion I sat her down and asked how things were going.

She told me she was after a new challenge and she had mastered her role. She had reduced the month end tasks from three days down to one and was now looking for the next challenge. When I asked her what was happening in these numbers she was clearly able to identify where the issues were and what was on and off track.

I asked her what she was doing to bring the off-track items back on track and understand and improve them. Her response was, "Nothing, my role is to pull together the figures and report them to the stakeholders who then decide what they need to do about it." When I pointed out that in five years' time AI and robots will be employed to do that for finance teams and that approach will see her make her role redundant, I finally had her attention.

For the next six months we deliberately and consciously got her involved with her stakeholders from a position of understanding what was driving the results, and working with them to help course-correct and resolve. At first she was nervous as she felt that she may be out of her depth and not have the required knowledge to assist, which is normal. However, these are business problems that nobody in the organisation has faced before, so she certainly would not be out of her depth. She just needed to inject herself into those conversations, add value, and impart her strong financial lens onto these problems in conjunction with the other departments knowledge.

Don't underestimate how easy it is to improve your credibility by just getting involved, observing and offering help in things that you may take for granted and assume others already know. Most of the time they don't know what you know.

In Section B: *Building Your Credibility* we will delve further into other techniques you can apply to improve your organisational acumen and Build Your Credibility.

Influence

The second dynamic that will define your success is your behaviours.

The things you say, the things you do and the style you have. Your body language, the words you use, how you turn up with other non-finance people within your organisation. This is where you build your influence within an organisation.

For a finance individual this normally looks like this:

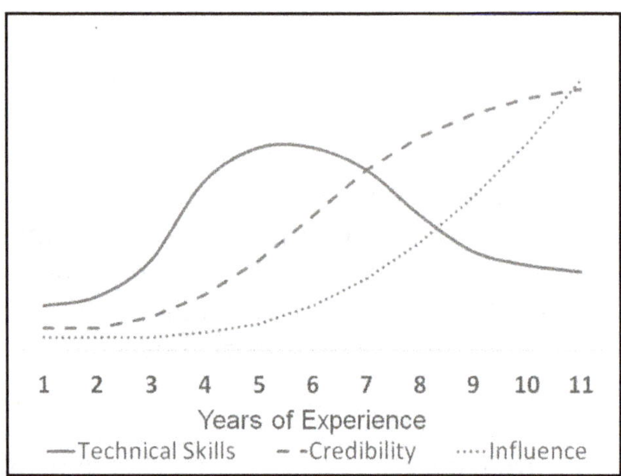

Figure 3: Influence curve

It builds slowly as most of us are meritocratic by nature (right/wrong, black/white) and then we start to understand that we need to be able to work with the other humans in an organisation who are not meritocratic. Once we realise this, it takes off quickly.

Now, as stupid as this sounds this behavioural line is a critical factor that can propel you quickly through an organisation and is often underestimated by finance people due to our meritocratic nature. It doesn't require much technical knowledge but does require a strong element of emotional intelligence or EQ.

Don't believe me. Surely, we get to the top of the organisation by being good at what we do most accountants believe. And in part it is true, but not 100% true.

Try to think of an individual in your organisation who always seems to get promoted or gets opportunities, but you look at them and think they do not seem to do a lot and don't seem to know anything. This is them.

The leaders of the organisation love them, and they behave in a way that's consistent with the people who have influence in the organisation. And they are technically inept.

It doesn't seem fair to us meritocratic, technically strong finance individuals. And it's not fair, but neither are organisations or politics.

This behavioural aspect of strong finance business partnering has four components:

1. Your team; leading them and working with the people who speak the language of finance and know what you are on about. How do you make sure the people you are leading are aligned and will do things for you as their leader? What behaviours are required to be successful at this?

2. Your peers; cross-functional people who are at your level or lower in the organisation but work in a completely different department that is not finance. Those who don't speak your language and speak their own language. How do you get to a place where you understand each other and can help each other? What behaviours are required to be successful at this?

3. Your stakeholders; your boss, your boss's boss, and your boss's peers. For your career aspirations to be fulfilled you need to know what they are looking for out of you and how do you influence them. What is your brand and reputation with them, because they will have a large say in your success. What are they saying about you in their meetings? What behaviours are required to be successful at this?

4. The organisation; how do the above three elements all come together and work in relation to the organisation you are in? Are you behaving in a way that is consistent with the leaders of the organisation and what do they want from you? If you want good work–life balance but the organisation you are in expects you to burn the midnight oil for them, how does this play out? What behaviours are required to be successful at this?

In Section C: *Influencing an Organisation* we will delve further into the first three of these areas (the fourth is difficult to assess without an understanding of specific organisations) and identify seven key behaviours required across these four lenses that will ensure success and build trust. And we will look at how some are more important than others, depending on who you are dealing with.

If you can influence your team, your peers and your stakeholders and build trust with them, then you are well on your way to becoming a successful finance business partner.

But to do so you have to have credibility first, and you have to do this "QUIET"ly.

The QUIET Approach to Finance Business Partnering

To be a strong finance business partner, you need to equip yourself with the correct skills and the right approach and style to apply those skills.

The QUIET Approach to finance business partnering is the framework utilised in the remainder of this book.

The word QUIET is used, as it is a nice acronym that can be remembered easily. It also sets the tone in which you need to do things to build your credibility, which in turn leads to your ability to influence an organisation.

Being QUIET refers to being measured, controlled, composed and considered. It is not about being absent, silent and not contributing. This is the style of a strong finance business partner rather than someone who is loud, combative, opinionated, obnoxious and arrogant about their skills and their function. Nobody in other functions likes that, and it makes you very difficult to "partner" with. The relationship will be out of balance.

It looks like this:

Figure 4: The QUIET Approach to Finance Business Partnering

"Quality" (Q) refers to ensuring that you and your team are producing information for your organisation that is of sound quality. In a recent study performed by our team, 42% of non-finance leaders (so CEOs, GMs, etc) indicated that the one thing they are looking for out of their finance team is accuracy. It rated almost twice as high as other things like business partnering, risk management, insights and governance. Delving further into these results it was noted there was approximately a 50/50 split for this being important because a) it is critical for the role/function of finance and b) these non-finance leaders felt that it wasn't currently being achieved by their finance teams. This is something which, as a finance community, we need to improve, and we can do this by ensuring the information we are producing (financial and non-financial) in our finance teams is of sound quality, free of error, relevant and reliable, but also that it is the information the organisation wants to see. Whether this is your own team or indirectly by a Centre of Excellence or centralised transactional team, as a finance business partner, and to ensure your credibility is maintained, you have an obligation to own the quality of information before it is released to the rest of the organisation.

"Understanding" (U) refers to building your organisational acumen. Within the organisation or environment you are in, you need to thoroughly understand how it works. How does it make money, what processes are working/not working, what role do you play within it, how does the value chain work to produce the products your organisation sells, to ultimately fulfil in meeting your customers' needs? Finance plays a key cross-functional role in understanding all of these elements and bringing them together for the benefit of the rest of the organisation.

"Insights" (I) is the ability to take the strong quality of information you have produced, and the organisational acumen you have, to go that one step further and provide meaningful and actionable insight and analysis from it (not just information). If you don't stay disciplined to the first two steps you risk producing insight or analysis that is not accurate and leads to the position above where non-finance leaders are questioning your accuracy. Historically, financial leaders spend a lot of time focused on costs and expenses to drive insight, but more and more the larger value is in how we help drive top line growth in our revenue and sales results.

From this stage you will have developed enough credibility to then move into the space of influencing your organisation.

"Ethos & Mindset" (E) is the term used to describe the mindset of a strong finance business partner. We are conditioned as accountants to be strong at the compliance and governance roles within our organisation, but as a strong finance business partner we need a different mindset. How do we stay true to the finance principles of integrity and objectivity but shift the dial slightly over to adding value with our business partners, and thinking in a slightly different way to create this value? We go through Six Key Principles of Finance Business Partnering which will help frame your mind toward success in this space.

"Trust" (T) is the final step in developing your ability to influence the organisation. How do you build trust within your finance team, your business partners (peers) and your stakeholders (your boss, your boss's boss and your boss's peers) to ensure they see value in what you are doing and are aligned to actioning the insights you are providing?

The five-step QUIET approach is a proven formula to success as a finance business partner. The first three steps (Quality, Understanding, Insight) talk to what is required to Build Your Credibility (Section B of this book), and the final two steps (Ethos, Trust) will help you to Influence an organisation (Section C).

Section B

Building Your Credibility

Q is for Quality

The first step toward becoming a strong finance business partner is ensuring you are producing, and are in control of, the quality of information that is available to the finance team, and then the organisation.

This information will predominantly be backward-looking and fact-based. In other words, it will most likely be actual results and will most often be financial in nature.

Please note: non-financial and forward-looking information is dealt with in "Insights" and is of even greater importance as a finance business partner, but for the purposes of building credibility we first need to start with ensuring there is quality information based on actuals and things that have happened as that is where people get their questions about business performance from.

Remember, you are in control of and have the choice...

Quality in... quality out.

Or, garbage in... garbage out.

You decide and control this. Irrespective of whether this is

- under your direct control as the leader of the team that produces most of the information; in larger organisations this is typically an FP&A role,
- is outsourced externally, or
- is under the control of a Centre of Excellence or centralised finance function within your organisation.

As a finance business partner, you ultimately have the responsibility to ensure the information is of adequate quality to be released to the wider business functions. Always consider it is you who will be held accountable if there is an error or there is questionable information. Not the people behind the scenes who are not "seen" by the rest of the organisation or who may be in another team within the wider finance structure, such as an FP&A or control team.

Keep in mind that the information you produce, or take to the organisation as Insight, will be wrong. It will either be wrong because it is either:

a) incorrect, or

b) it is not the result the organisation wants it to be.

You don't want it to be the first of these.

A sign it is a) is when somebody puts something up on a

presentation and the room full of people spend time debating whether the information on the screen is correct, rather than talking about the underlying insight.

As a finance business partner, you have a responsibility to ensure you are always talking about b) and not a). Accordingly, investment needs to be made in this space. As the person in charge of producing and interpreting the financial information of the organisation you need to take full and complete ownership of ensuring the people, systems and processes behind the scenes that lead into your ledger and out of your ledger are functioning correctly.

Does this add value? Not directly, but without it you will be leaving it up to luck to ensure your credibility. Which is ok for some, and I have seen some accountants succeed relying on luck. But I have seen more fail due to relying on luck. The penalty for that is your credibility will come into question, which often leads to you having to leave the organisation and start again in order to correct it (either immediately or after a few years of frustration at not being able to gain back your credibility).

So how does this manifest itself within an organisation?

First, we will talk about how finance effectiveness works (directly and indirectly). We will introduce the language of “left hand circle” and “right hand circle” thinking. Then we will move to addressing the “seesaw” or balancing act required to ensure you are not only producing good quality information (that is most likely historic) but also adding value (by providing insight on future information). Trying to get information 100% correct is a goal but it’s not effective. It takes your time away from using that information to provide insight and direction. And that is the space most finance business partners want to add value in and is also where our non-finance business partners want us to add value, the forward-looking insights space.

Spend too little time on quality, and you won't be able to provide relevant and reliable insight.

Spend too much time on it and you won't have time to provide relevant and reliable insight.

It is a balancing act that needs to be managed.

Left Hand Circle, Right Hand Circle work

As a Finance Business Partner you will often be confronted with a choice or judgment when you are working within an organisation.

That judgment predominantly comes down to two choices of where you spend your time. Do you:

a. rely on the financial information provided by colleagues/ systems and get to work on identifying opportunities for the organisation (and add value immediately)?

   OR

b. spend time ensuring the integrity and credibility of that information you are relying on is adequate and the environment it comes from is operating effectively (and adding value at a slower pace and indirectly)?

Visually, do you spend time on the "left hand circles" or the "right hand circles" of the below framework.

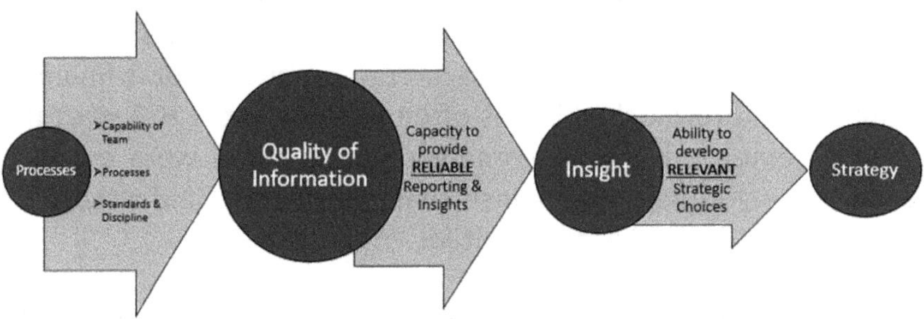

Figure 5: Finance Effectiveness Circles

Moving forward and throughout this book we will refer to the above as left hand circle work (processes that produce quality information) and right hand circle work (insights and adding value).

Unfortunately, when dealing with most GMs, CEOs or owners, or non-finance people, the right hand circle work is the reason they have employed you, and the left hand circle work is assumed to be under control. They would most likely not consider that the quality of information would be an issue (and nor should they). It's assumed by non-finance people this would never be a problem.

Accordingly, for finance people the right hand circle work is why they became a business partner and is "sexier" and more engaging than the left hand circle work. It is also one of the major subtleties faced by accountants leaving professional services and going into a commercial organisation. How do you balance the amount of work required to produce quality information with the amount of time required to produce insight and add direct value (left hand circles work versus right hand circle work)? As an accountant who may have recently left the professional services game and started within a commercial organisation it can be a shock to understand the amount of work required to simply produce sound financial results when previously this was often just presented to you at the commencement of any assignment or project you were engaged to do. Now you have to cleanse that information and ensure its accuracy (or another team does it for you).

The right hand circle work also has tangible returns immediately, and helps to justify the somewhat expensive cost of a senior finance business partner. Fair enough I say.

Left hand circle work is indirect, nobody outside of finance sees it as adding value, and they assume it just happens. Right hand circle work has more direct value. Non-finance see value in the right hand side.

Left hand circle work is spent on transactions, and accounting for and capturing them. Right hand circle work is future-looking, like forecasting, budgets, strategic plans and predicting what's going on. Non-finance see value in the right hand side.

Left hand circle work is more certain, it has happened, and we should really know what it looks like. Right hand circle work is more ambiguous, complex and high level. Non-finance see value in the right hand side.

Left hand circle work should be automated and time spent on it reduced as much as possible. Right hand circle work is where you need to be spending your time and freeing up resources to be spent here. Why? Because (in case you haven't noticed the trend) non-finance see value in the right hand side.

As mentioned previously, a recent study showed 42% of senior (non-finance) managers and execs say the biggest thing they want from their finance team is "accuracy". It is not business partnering skills, it is not insight, and it is not risk management.

It is accuracy.

As a senior finance individual who takes the integrity of any information and advice I provide as critical to my reputation and success, I find it hard to believe that this is not a given for all finance teams. The results of this study also hypothesised that the real reason for this high score is not because it is important in itself, but because GMs, CEOs and owners are not currently getting the desired level of "accuracy" from their finance teams. And as a consultant who experiences different environments on a regular basis and is asked to consult on finance business partnering, I can confirm that it is most likely a left hand side issue that needs attention.

So, can we provide more value by identifying areas for financial improvement from the information provided (right hand circle work), and/or can we add more value by reducing the 42% of senior managers who feel they aren't getting accurate information from their finance team (left hand circle work)?

The answer is likely to be both. And one leads to the other.

The “Insights” section of this book is where the right hand circle work of the above framework starts and is where you confirm your Credibility within an organisation and start to Influence.

But before we get there we want to ensure the “system” is operating effectively (the left hand circle work). If this isn’t working, you risk your business partners questioning the credibility of the information you provide. At the very least things will be inefficient and take you longer than they should. As soon as that happens, you put at risk any chance of adding value with them, as it gives them a chance to question your figures and avoid accountability.

The three areas of the left hand side that need your attention are Capability of Team (People), Processes, and Standards & Discipline. These will be specific to every organisation and are fluid in that they can change from time to time – i.e. you don’t fix one and find it remains fixed forever, it will constantly be moving.

Capability of Team (People)

The capability of not only the team under your control, but the wider finance team you influence and the non-finance members of your organisation that input information is a key factor in the ability to produce sound quality information. Poor capability leads to poor quality. So how can you ensure the various members of an organisation who input information into systems that ultimately end up in your ledger are performing to an adequate level for you to produce quality financial information?

Set expectations; consistently and relentlessly reinforce and communicate your expectations of what is required from them. If people do not understand what you expect and the consequences of doing things incorrectly they will never improve or perform at the standard expected. Especially for non-finance people who are processing purchase orders, coding things wrong, performing poor calculations to support journals or analysis, etc. – they need to know why they should care (WDIC? – why do I care?) and what's in it for them (WIIFM? – what's in it for me?). Communicate to them via these two lenses to ensure they understand the importance of their responsibilities and your conversations will be more along the lines of praising them for good work (really easy to do) instead of critiquing them for poor work (more difficult to do).

Follow up; many times you will request for someone to do something and nothing happens. They don't bother or they "forget". This can be infuriating to a finance person, but the reality is that often it is because the person you have asked simply hasn't prioritised this as important in "their" world. Accordingly, the best mechanism to negate this is follow up. Agree timelines and follow up if they are not met, and follow it up on the timelines you set, not a day or a week later. If you have agreed a timeline with someone and they have not met it and not communicated with you, then follow up will ensure the chances of this happening again in the future will be reduced. If I know I have agreed to do something with someone by Friday, and I don't, and they come to me on Friday asking me where it is, I feel I have let them down. Next time I will ensure it gets done or at the very least communicate why I have not met the agreed timelines. And the beauty of follow up is that the earlier and more times you do it, the less you will have to later as the tone will have been set.

Reward and reprimand; if people understand what is expected of them then the next step to ensure strong performance is to praise them when they do it well, and reprimand them when they don't. In order to do this effectively you need to be specific about your feedback – you need to provide examples, blend positive and negative feedback together and provide alternatives if you do not agree.

The above is a very simple three-step framework for ensuring the people in your team, your wider finance colleagues and other functions will perform the correct processes that create quality information. It is important to note none of the above addresses building strong relationships, rapport and trust with them. This will be addressed further in the "Trust" section.

Processes

Avoid Rework; the number one enemy of any finance team is rework. Identifying a problem, then going back and reversing it, then fixing and doing it again all takes a lot longer than getting it done right the first time. It is why some finance teams work until midnight and others leave at 5 pm. In addition, the work done at midnight is of no apparent value to anyone outside of finance. They will often ask "What are they doing in finance?" Most of the time it is because you are fixing things that have been done incorrectly – rework. To reduce rework, build in preventative and detective controls so that you pick them up beforehand. If things are of high risk and high potential to be incorrect, check them before they are processed (preventative). For small items with minimal impact, don't worry about them, review them post-processing (detective). The role of finance business partner is hard enough without having to do it twice.

Know your "One source of truth"; more often than not this should and will be your ledger. But the ledgers of all accounting systems these days are linked to many other systems and reports. Review the reporting, management and measurement systems that "hang off" the ledger you are relying on and ensuring you know where your "one source of truth" is and who is in control of it. Quite often these supporting systems will only capture part of the information that makes up the complete financial system. It is imperative that you understand what is included, and what isn't included in these systems. In a recent client I visited they had a financial ledger that reported a gross margin of 43%, however the management reporting system they used to manage the performance of their business showed 49%. In a $30m business, a total of $1.8m in expenditure was not being looked at simply because it was being coded to cost centres and accounts that had not been configured in the management reporting system. Now that does not particularly add any value directly, but improving the processes and the back end to ensure that $1.8m is being analysed and insight provided is a good start. Especially if it has never been looked at previously. It will also help to reduce the 42% of senior managers who feel "accuracy" is the most important thing they require from their finance team. Is it little wonder they feel this way when one report says 49% margin, and the other says 43% and nobody is doing anything about it outside of blaming IT?

Stop doing things; the easiest way to work out if processes and controls are working efficiently is to stop doing them. Often a lot of tasks done within a finance team within an organisation are done because "That is how we have always done it." Over years many tasks just keep getting built upon with no consideration as to whether the business is actually getting any benefit out of it. I'm not suggesting stopping doing everything (there will be some tasks and reports you should know the business needs and uses) but if you are unsure as to why you are doing something, just stop doing them. By suddenly not doing some of these tasks you will quickly find out who is using them (as they will ask where it is) and you will quickly find out why they are using it. You may find nobody even asks in which case you have just saved yourself some time. Try doing this for the reports you provide the business each month by taking out one page you suspect nobody is using, each month. If nobody uses it, it won't be missed. If someone does need it, they will most likely come to you after three or four months and ask about it, in which case you can suggest doing it quarterly, in line with how they use it. Again, saving some time to add value elsewhere.

Discipline/Standards

The accuracy of the information the finance team produces is entirely up to you. Non-finance individuals do not understand the intricacies of systems and reporting and how things mesh together each month/quarter. Accordingly, it is your (or your teams) responsibility to ensure it does. Nobody else will. All they will find is the errors you potentially make and will lead them to question the credibility of any information you provide. Even if it was caused by someone in another department not following protocol. It is your responsibility to detect this and correct it before others see it. You can only do this by maintaining a high level of standards and not accepting sub-par information.

The lowest level of standard you accept, is the highest level of standard you can expect.

Never apologise for having high standards, people will rise to them if you create the right environment and understanding for them.

Always keep in mind if you don't get the "left hand circles" correct, you will damage your credibility and ability to get your foot in the door to do the "right hand circles".

As a Finance Business Partner this is the dilemma you will often face within an organisation. We don't deliver front line sales, we don't make things, and we are a cost. But we can certainly add value from providing insight (right side circles), improving the effectiveness and efficiency of the systems that produce this insight (left side circles), and most importantly improve the "accuracy" question that can hang over a finance department.

Enemies of Quality

Through the research we have performed there are several recurring themes that occur in any finance team which contribute to poor quality information. These themes come through any team that is struggling to get out of the left hand circle work and over to the right hand circle work. Accordingly keep these concepts in the back of your mind while you work through producing historical information and avoid them as much as possible.

Rework – reworking errors means wasted time. If there is an error, you will need to spend time working out the problem, reversing the error and correcting it. Get it right the first time and avoid correcting and reworking things. Rework has double jeopardy if you have to rework something that is picked up by someone else as an error. Not only will you waste time reworking, your credibility with that person will be in question. To avoid this, ensure you have in place detection and prevention mechanisms that pick things up before they break.

Time – we all could use some more time to do things. Unfortunately, time does not change and is a fixed predetermined concept. We can't create more, and we can't lose any. It is the same every hour of every day of every week. Accordingly, being disciplined to the time you spend on things and moving on when they are near enough is ok. Being perfect and wasting time is not ok. We simply do not have enough time to do everything in finance so prioritise the important and risky.

Detailed Reporting – we are all proud of producing a large deck with lots of charts, tables and information in for all the world to see. Unfortunately, the majority of the world doesn't look at it. And if they do, detailed reporting will lead to detailed questions which may or may not be issues. Jumping at shadows is often caused by too much information. Take a page out of your reporting deck each month and see if anyone notices. If they don't you don't have to do it again. If they do, just apologise and include it next time. Password protect your management reports to see if anyone is using them (seriously, try this). The worst thing that can happen is that you now know why you are producing the information.

Manual Processes – automate everything you can. Manual processes done by humans bring into focus the chance of an error. Manual spreadsheets even more so. Wherever you can, automate processes and reporting to avoid this enemy. This is where the industry is going through RPA and AI and where accountants need to move away from if they are to add value and keep their role in an organisation.

Systems and People – someone outside of finance will always have done something to influence your numbers. Non-finance people doing finance things, like accruals. Systems can also produce some odd numbers that don't flow through accurately. Review other functions inputs and ensure systems work correctly or are being reviewed.

Priorities – you will often be faced with the dilemma of juggling competing priorities. Everyone wants their finance business partner to help them. You need to prioritise and manage that with them. Understanding context helps to direct your priorities and communicating it is critical so people understand why you have or haven't done something.

Surprises – you perform all your tasks and processes and yet produce a result that doesn't make sense. It doesn't feel right. Nothing kills your credibility more than surprises. Accordingly start with an end in mind. What do you think it's going to look like, based on your understanding of what has happened? If it doesn't match up, ensure you understand why. Never explain what you have done by explaining the process. To avoid surprises, increase the conversations you have with people to keep on top of things regularly.

If you can avoid or minimise the above enemies of good quality, you will be able to minimise the chance of your credibility being questioned.

Following the above framework of "Left hand circle, right hand circle" work will now hopefully have helped in balancing the seesaw of quality and priorities. You will have managed to produce

"Quality Information" – that is generally backward-looking, and actual and transactional based. It shouldn't take too long to do this as it is known and unambiguous.

The next step in the QUIET approach is to ensure you "Understand your Role and the Organisation" so you can bring this alive and navigate effectively within it.

U is for Understanding

The role of a Finance Business Partner is somewhat different to an accountant within an organisation. Financial Accounting is different to Management Accounting. Trusted advisor to other functions within the organisation is different to a control and governance role within an organisation. Many accountants struggle with this when they make the transition from practice to industry or when they make the transition internally, i.e. moving from a financial reporting or internal assurance role to a commercial business partnering role.

In order to be effective in this space a finance person needs to understand:

- their role (as a business partner),
- the organisation they are in and how it operates,
- the people in the organisation and how they operate (mainly non-finance).

This chapter and the "U" of "Understanding" addresses these three dynamics.

Your Role (Compliance to Commercial)

All accountants are conditioned to behave and think a certain way. It is drilled into us when we do our formal education, and then go through the rigours of our professional membership exams. Things like integrity, objectivity, due care, competence, conflict of interest are all terms that form the basis of the oath we all agree to when becoming accountants. It is in our charter and our by-laws, we can't escape them. This also leads into a significant portion of the work we do in society in professional services and in a large portion of a finance department within an organisation. Tax returns, financial statements, audits, insolvency are all areas and tasks that require an individual to think in a certain way. And the aforementioned characteristics fit nicely with these.

Let's never forget we are qualified accountants with extremely strong technical skills working within organisations.

Unfortunately to be a strong business partner, where we are working with individuals who may not have these qualities instilled into them, we need to be thinking in a slightly different way. We are there to "partner" them and assist them in helping the business to unlock opportunities.

Put simply, we are there to help make the organisation more money, or save them more money, reach their strategic objectives and achieve their KPIs

How we report it, how it is treated, the lines you report it on and the laws of accounting and tax are irrelevant when we are trying to increase your organisations bank account and key lead measurements for this. We can all be very creative in our accounting. We can defer items, bring forward items and justify these adequately within the frameworks of the accounting profession. But in the end if we are not helping our organisation make money or save money, and hit their objectives, then our job becomes one of reporting, controls and governance, roadblocks and minimal value add in the eyes of our constituents (business partners).

So, if the mindset of the typical accountant is one of checking, compliance, reviewing, governing, etc., what does this force us to think like? Often, we will be considered or be thinking like a policeman. Someone who has the laws of the game and keeps everyone in the organisation accountable to them. If you step out of line, you will be punished, if you work within the laws you will be allowed to continue but you certainly won't be rewarded, well not by the finance department anyway.

And this mindset of the policeman is not helpful or effective if we want to be a great finance business partner.

So, if the mindset of the policeman, the person who keeps everyone accountable, and the values of the profession which have been instilled into you don't work, then what does. Let's consider some basic analogies and metaphors that can help, because metaphors are a great way to bring context to things.

Goalkeeper

A great analogy or metaphor to consider for any finance business partner is that of a goalkeeper in a soccer team. This concept needs to be considered in the context of the other players of the team to be effective.

As a finance business partner, you are not the strikers, you are not the midfielders. You may be the backs but above all you are the goalkeeper. And being comfortable and understanding of this is important. The strikers will get paid more money, they will get recognised and get all the glory more than the goalkeeper (often like sales may in an organisation). You need to be comfortable with this. Because your role is something different, you are the goalkeeper. The last line of defence so that if something goes wrong everywhere else you will be there to protect them.

You sit in a position where you have access to more information than anyone else in the organisation. Financial information, industry statistics, competitor data, etc. are all at your fingertips. Like a goalkeeper in a football match. Everything is in front of you. You have the best seat in the house to see what is on track and off track. Are players in position, is the opposition vulnerable or strong in certain positions? You can see this better than anybody else, and potentially better than the team manager on the sidelines (or the CEO in their corner office). And it is your obligation to be communicating these things to your teammates. If you don't, then you will be left exposed when things come your way that haven't worked very well. In a football match this may mean the goalkeeper being left one-on-one with the opposition's striker and the last line of defence to make a save. For a finance business partner this may mean picking up on a KPI or financial piece of information that isn't in the place it needs to be, and if you are passive in either situation then the inevitable will occur. A goal against, or money out the door for your organisation.

Another important issue to cope with is the concept that sometimes finance business partnering is just a really, really busy place in an organisation. Like a goalkeeper, that time is often when things are not working well, and the pressure and questions just seem to keep coming. Like in a football match, if your team is not performing well or is up against strong opposition it is highly likely that the goalkeeper is going to be very busy. Either saving goals or picking them out of the net. In a match you are losing 5–0, you are likely to be very busy as a goalkeeper. Likewise, a finance business partner is likely to be very busy if the business isn't performing. Don't be afraid of this or complain about it, instead use it as the opportunity to influence and help navigate the business through. When the business is not performing as expected, finance will be asked to do some significant pieces of work to determine what is going on and recommend and manage ways out of it.

On the flipside, when the football team is 5–0 up and winning the goalkeeper probably isn't going to be required to do much. The ball isn't coming down a lot, the ball seems to be up the other end a lot. Things seem a lot easier. This is similar for finance in an organisation that is achieving its goals. Questions that come across your desk are easier to deal with, you have the structures in place to respond with pace and life seems to have less pressure. Unfortunately, the only way to get to that space is through hard work, being good at what you do, and having the entire organisation/team playing their role effectively.

The final point in relation to this metaphor is that you are expected to make as few mistakes as possible, because when you do they are impactful. Search google for footage of goalkeepers making mistakes and the impact on the team is massive. Likewise, when finance makes a mistake, or something isn't picked up it can have a large impact on the organisation, from fraud to lost opportunity to costing the company money. We have a thankless task, and often nobody says well done when we do our role, but if we make a mistake we are certainly told about it. Like a goalkeeper. Even in a penalty shootout where the keeper has made a save or two, people will often remember the person who missed or kicked the winning/losing goal. But sometimes, you are the hero and being ready when the time comes is critical.

Unfortunately, that is our role. Accept it and play your role. If you want to be a hero and get the glory, become a striker. If you want to be a better finance business partner, be a goalkeeper.

Pilot

A second metaphor to think about when becoming a finance business partner is that of a pilot or a co-pilot. A pilot is at the steering wheel of a remarkable machine and has the responsibility to put that machine 30,000 ft in the air, fly safely, land it at its destination and most importantly deliver all their passengers there, preferably incident free, and definitely alive.

In the cockpit the pilot has all the information at their fingertips that tells them whether things are working, or things are not working. This is someone who has a lot of information at their disposal and is entrusted to act accordingly if there is anything that goes wrong.

Like a finance business partner. The cockpit is like a dashboard. A lot of information on it, some relevant some not so relevant. Some important at certain times and some important at other times. The pilot's job is to navigate this information, distil it, and act accordingly. Sometimes this can be easy sometimes this can be difficult. Just like a finance business partner who has access to a lot of financial information and non-financial information and needs to know what is relevant and what is not. When the red light starts to flash on the dashboard, is this important and how urgently does something need to happen to course correct. Can it be fixed, can it be mitigated, does it need escalation?

Unfortunately, sometimes that responsibility comes with a level of self-importance, where you feel like you want to impart your wisdom on others to ensure they know you are over it. But it doesn't really help. Think of a time when you were on a plane, you've been away on business and you are keen to return home safely. It's been a long few days away on business. The pilot comes on and says:

> 'Good evening ladies and gentlemen and welcome aboard flight 123 to Sydney. Today we are going to head out over the west runway, go out over the bay and make a quick left turn before rising to 30,000 ft. We are heading into quite a strong headwind which means we may be slightly later than normal, but we hope to be disembarking at your destination in Sydney no later than five minutes late.'

You think to yourself that's wonderful information but is it relevant to me? I don't really care, just fly the plane, get it up in the air, get it down, keep it safe and ensure I arrive home alive. Everything else is irrelevant to me outside of "Please don't stuff up and we all die."

This is what a being a finance business partner can be like. Being comfortable with that is important. Nobody cares about accounting standards and tax laws, they only care if it means something to them and has an impact. I certainly don't want to know about the technical aspects of a pilot's job – I just want him to fly me to my destination in one piece. Outside of that I only want to know what's relevant. This is what people think of finance, it might be exciting to you but to others this is difficult and complex stuff they often shy away from. Numbers can be difficult for some people. They don't care, just deal with stuff for them. For other functions most of things you may have to say at any one time is just noise for them and not business critical in their world.

Another concept a pilot is great at is to become comfortable in the space where often nobody thanks you for doing your job. Like a goalkeeper. Nobody thanks a pilot for getting us there safely, it's just their job. Sometimes when the plane lands safely you may have a group of people who clap or say "phew" we arrived safely. But the pilot doesn't hear that. He is locked behind closed doors in the cockpit. Even if you wanted to thank him nobody goes in there and says, "Thanks Captain you really did a good job getting us here alive today."

It's the same in finance. People expect you to deal with the information and respond. They certainly don't thank you. They expect you to identify issues and provide solutions to them. Sometimes unfortunately working in finance is a thankless task. That is normal and the best finance people accept and deal with it. Even when sometimes you feel like you are being held responsible for something that you have simply stumbled across. Just like a pilot. Captain Sullenberger of flight 1549 must have felt this way when his decision to drop a plane into the Hudson River ultimately led to the line in the movie *Sully* – "I've delivered a million passengers over 40 years in the air and in the end, I'll be judged on 208 seconds."

Don't underestimate that it is a tough gig, finance. Business partnering is challenging. You are expected to see the world through every function's lens. But it is very rewarding and certainly adds value to an organisation if done well.

Your Organisation (Organisational Acumen)

Once you understand your role as a Finance Business Partner it should become apparent that applying your knowledge in an organisation can only be done if you understand that organisation and how it works. Every organisation is different and does things in different ways. Coca Cola and Pepsi are predominantly organisations selling the same things, but the way their organisations operate are completely different.

Fundamental to getting this understanding is to get away from your desk and get involved in the organisation. Sitting behind your desk absorbed in spreadsheets will provide a superficial understanding of the business but it will not create the depth required to find those gold nuggets you need to be an effective finance business partner. People have been in your organisation for several years working on it and in it every day over that time. They have found all the gold nuggets that come rolling down the river. In order to add value, you need to get the pan out and start panning for gold in the river bed and potentially finding some "little" specks of gold. Those 1%ers make you valuable in your organisation.

How does it make money?

The first step in "understanding" your organisation is to get a deep and thorough understanding of how it makes money. How does it transfer all of its inputs into outputs for its customers?

The easiest and most common way to break this down is through a value chain analysis as described by Michael Porter[1]. This is a very thorough approach to determining how you make money and will also identify inefficiencies in the process of turning inputs into outputs. Unfortunately, that can be quite time-consuming when you have daily deliverables so to break this down attempt to answer the following questions as a starting point:

- What KPIs are leading and lagging and which are the most important based on the language and actions within the organisation?

- How does your organisation balance volume versus profit?

- What are the specific mechanisms the organisation uses to drive volume/share?

- How structured is the organisation in relation to policies around the above?

- Is there a strong correlation between cash and profit? If not, how is the path between these managed, what can you influence (think of a retailer where the timing of cash and profit are similar versus a property company where

1. See, Porter, Michael E. (1985) *Competitive Advantage* (NY: Free Press)

there is a large difference between the timing of cash and profit)?

- What sort of things does the business do when it is chasing targets (balancing short-term tactical decisions with long term tactical decisions)?

- What are the largest and most variable expenses within the organisation? Why are they like that and what drives them, and can they be managed down/up?

- What costs get cut first in times of downturn?

The above is not an exhaustive list in any way but by answering these questions you will start to paint a picture of where the organisation goes and how it behaves when times are good/bad. It will also help to identify the things the executive team may be talking about around the board table. If you do not know how the company makes money and what it does under pressure you will not have a great understanding of where you need to inject yourself to add the most value.

Getting involved

"Getting involved" is a term used to describe the act of getting away from your desk and your spreadsheets and getting out into the business. Spending time with the human resources of the organisation and understanding how their world works, and how you may be able to assist them in achieving their goals – how do you partner them?

As a guide, if you are not currently doing this, target at least one day a month being out of the office with your business partners, with a goal of that being one day a week (it may take you some time to free up your current workload to support this).

"Getting involved" can take two forms

- "Learning" from your Business Partners,

- "Teaching" your Business Partners.

The first of these ("Learning") is self-explanatory. Any opportunity you get to go out into the business and spend time with your business partners is one you should grab with both hands. Be this spending time with a sales person, going to a customer negotiation, having an ideation session with marketing, scoping a project with IT, visiting a manufacturing plant. All of these are quite basic ways of spending time in functions that are foreign to you, so that you can understand what is going on.

But it's not simply a matter of turning up and being passive. In order to learn as much as you can you need to have a curious mind. A lot of literature is written on having curiosity. This is an:

"Appetite to Understand"

Are you inherently motivated to wanting to understand what is going on in other functions of your organisation?

If you cannot answer yes to that, I would suggest you move to a transactional or reporting finance role.

Please Note: Due to the importance of this concept, "Appetite to Understand" is addressed further in the "Ethos" section where techniques to do this are discussed.

The benefits of going out into your organisation, spending time with your Business Partners and asking questions to improve your understanding are quite subtle and often intangible. As much as you will get direct benefit by improving your understanding, and learning what can go wrong, what works well, what impacts different parts of the business, etc., you will also start to build your credibility in the eyes of your business partner.

You will also start to build strong relationships with the people in your organisation. And as much as we move to an automated world, business is still fundamentally about people and the human experience. They will be grateful for having you with them and taking the time to understand their world and you will have begun to build a relationship with someone you previously didn't have. And you never know, they may mention the time you spent with them with their superiors which can only further enhance your credibility within the organisation.

The second aspect of "Getting Involved" is "Teaching" your Business Partners.

Do not underestimate the knowledge and skills that you have as a Finance Business Partner. You have access to information others do not see on a daily basis (Knowledge). That could be financial like sales, budgets, costs, etc. Not a lot of people in the organisation have this. People are often curious to how the organisation is going so share what you can with them (being conscious of confidentiality).

Other functions also do not have the skills that you have. Things as simple as mathematics others find very difficult to do, whereas you find it easy. My sister-in-law will ring or text me two or three times a year asking me to perform a % calculation for her. It takes me two seconds and I can often do it in my head. But she finds it difficult. Now, do I blame her for this or get frustrated about it. No, I help her and do something I find easy. She thinks I am the smartest man she knows. And in return I ask her to provide fashion tips for me (because that's what she is good at and I am not). It's a great partnership.

Your Excel skills should also not be underestimated. Things like pivot tables, macros and sumifs are things we take for granted. Other functions do not use these on a daily basis. So, use these skills to your advantage and show others how they can get the best out of the programs we use. I was once asked to review the processes in a warehouse team. Within ten minutes I had identified that someone was spending 45 minutes a day, printing off a list and retyping it into another program. I showed this person the simple function of copy and paste and had saved them 45 minutes a day. They were amazed, and thought I was wonderful. And even better, they told their boss with no context how I had saved her close to an hour a day, and her boss told his boss and suddenly, they thought I was adding so much value without even knowing the simple help I had provided.

The "Others" (Non Finance People)

As a Finance Business Partner, the majority of your time is going to be spent working with other functions. If you are successful as a Finance Business Partner and your infrastructure supports it, more of your time will be spent with other functions than with Finance.

We call these people "The Others" and in order to be a successful Finance Business Partner you need to be able to:

"Speak Their Language"

Just like in the television series Lost our initial feelings of these "Others" is that they are a threat and that we don't understand them. That thought needs to be broken down, so we can see "The Others" as our allies and the people we can learn from and teach, so that true business partnering can occur.

Accordingly, it is important to be able to understand the way those other functions think about the world and how they approach their role within an organisation.

The success of you as a Finance Business Partner is widely measured by the success of "The Others" department too.

Due to the importance of understanding this as a mindset, the "Ethos" section of this book talks to this some more under the section "Speak Their Language".

In addition, we also spend time in the "Trust" section on Working Cross-Functionally.

Accordingly, this section of the book is only here to highlight and introduce to you the concept that understanding "The Others" is critically important if you want to be a successful finance business partner.

If you do not "Understand" how they think about the world, the pressures they have and what they are looking from you as a finance partner to them, achieving success with them is going to be difficult.

Just like any organisation that produces a product or service, if it doesn't fulfil the needs of the customer then its likelihood of success is reduced. For a Finance Business Partner, not understanding what your business partners in other functions want from you, will reduce your chance of being successful. Don't give them what you think they need or want, give them what they think they need or want from a finance perspective.

As mentioned this is addressed in further detail in Ethos and Trust.

You are now in a position where your credibility will be building. You have structured your team and processes to produce "Quality" information that is relevant and reliable for the organisation. You have also started to inject yourself into the business to "Understand" how it works. You are aware your role as a Finance Business Partner is slightly different to that of a classical accountant, you know how your organisation works and how the people in it operate. This will place you in a strong position to continue to build your credibility and start to place you in a position where you can provide some forward looking "Insight".

I is for Insight

Now that we have improved the "Quality" of information you are producing, and you have a strong "Understanding" of the organisation you are working in, it is time to move from "left hand circle" work and into the space of "right hand circle" work. Your credibility within the organisation will have grown to an appropriate level where you can now start to influence it and you don't have to rely on luck.

However, it is important to ensure you start to provide Insight and not just information. The abundance of information available to most accountants has driven this need to analyse, interpret and understand almost everything within an organisation… and to provide insight on that information.

So how does an accountant respond to the constant challenge from other departments for "more insight" when our training revolves around a world that is objective, merit-based and chiselled down to an answer? Black or white? Yes or No? We spend years studying and doing exams that condition us to be like this. A right or a wrong answer. A little bit of subjectivity, and a lot of objectivity. And accordingly, when asked for insight, a lot of us do the right thing and provide information. Reports that show variances or, for the developed, some form of traffic light (Green = Good, Red = Bad).

Is this really insight??? Or is it just a sophisticated form of information?

Sadly, our industry is often regarded as being a group of information providers, rather than providing real insight and understanding, and influence an organisation to act and respond accordingly. That is the place we as accountants need to get to if we want businesses and organisations to take our functional roles seriously and show that we can add real value beyond the administrative functions most other departments think we only do. We need to do more "right hand circle" work and less "left hand circle" work.

So how do we do this? The following step-by-step approach should help in moving you up the spectrum of information provider to insight delivery. And as a bonus (in Step 3), what to be thinking of to bring that insight out to your various stakeholders.

Step 1: Gather the information (What is the Information?)

The first step in providing value added insight is to gather the information to work with. And to have systems and processes in place that do this quickly, and accurately. This is ***basic level finance*** and for some departments begins and ends here. Month-end reporting, profitability analysis, variance analysis is all information gathering. Providing commentary that says "x product is 8% below budget" is just a restatement of information. It is not insight. This step needs to be done accurately and efficiently. Minimise the time on this (potentially outsource it or automate it), so that more time can be spent analysing it and adding value, rather than checking it is accurate, reworking and correcting it, and pulling it into a workable form.

Step 2: Identify the "so what" (What does it mean?)

A sound and ***intermediate finance team*** does this. They will take the information provided in Step 1 and review it with a critical eye to identify things that look unusual (good or bad) and spend the time on understanding why. A good level of understanding of the business, and having the right conversations, will help to provide some form of "so what" to the information you are providing. When you get the response from someone "that's interesting" you have probably moved yourself to this level. You have gathered some information, analysed it and identified something that has captured people's attention. Stopping there will identify you as a strong finance individual within your organisation. But if you want to be a strong commercial person, there is one last step...

Step 3: What are we doing about it?

This is where it gets complex and is a level only the ***advanced business partner*** will get to. What to do about it could be obvious, or it could be caught up in a myriad of alternatives. With more than one right answer. This requires you to not only think about the company you are in, but the conflicting aspects of that company. What impact will anything you do have on your customers? What will your competitors think, and respond with?

As an example, you identify in your review that personnel costs are 10% over budget:

Gather the information – personnel costs are 10% over budget

What does this mean? – they are 10% over budget because…

What are we doing about it? – if this continues it looks like… and course correction opportunities include…

Picture yourself on a yacht heading out of Sydney, with the final destination Fiji. You have planned for this trip, reviewed the weather, ensured the yacht is capable of the journey, etc., and you set sail. But as you head out of the harbour and sail into the night the conditions change. The weather is completely different and you suffer significant damage to your boat.

"An accountant" tells you all the information you need to know about what happened.

A "good finance person" tells you that if things continue going the way they are going you will probably end up in New Zealand, or at worst sink.

A "great finance business partner" finds opportunities for insight and to add value to the situation and helps you get to Fiji.

The 3 C's

"What are we doing about it" we call The **3 C's** and being able to view the information you have provided that is interesting through these three lenses will contribute to making good decisions about what you do next.

Company – What does the information you have gathered and analysed mean for your company, from all aspects? This should be able to be gathered with some degree of confidence. Financial, operational, human resources, market share, etc. All of these metrics and influences are active within an organisation, every day of every week. And a lot of these metrics conflict with each other, and a choice is often needed as to what is most important. And that choice could be different one week versus another. A perfect example of this is where a choice needs to be made between making profit or gaining share. Which one do you choose? Well, it depends. Sometimes share is important at the expense of some profit. And sometimes profit is more important. And next week it could be the opposite. In the long run both are important, but at any point in time one may be more so. Your decision could impact staff, it could impact manufacturing capacity which flows into unit costs. The list is endless but forcing yourself to think of these things from an entire company perspective will assist in determining what you do about it.

HINT: you may have to talk to several people in other departments before you get a solid handle on this.

Customer – Your customers are also critical to any decisions you make. In the end this is why you are in business and keeping them feeling like they are receiving value from your products and services is critical. You will have a fair idea of what your customers will do in response (if not you, then your sales team will) but you have little control over it. What will their response be to any action we take from this insight? How is our relationship with them, is there anything we can leverage in any discussions we have with them? Anything to do with customers that changes the status quo will involve a negotiation, and a negotiation involves give and take and leverage. They also have context and an environment they live in that you need to consider. You may or may not be aware of what that is, so spend some time attempting to understand it with fact (rather than anecdotal knowledge) so it does not blindside you and prepare to be challenged by them. Remember, without your customers you make no money.

Competitors – Then we have our competitors. Organisations that are trying to win our business and will always be on the look-out for our signals with which they will respond. This "C" is the C you will have little or no control over and your knowledge may be assumption-based. Accordingly, the signals you send need to be subtle if you do not want to encourage a response from them. War games and competitor days where you put yourself in the shoes of your competitor to attempt to determine what they are thinking are a great way of getting insight into this. Be thorough, but don't jump to conclusions or biases. You will never have perfect information in this space, so a "balance of probabilities" and a risk-mitigation approach to what they may do is recommended.

Please note: *For consumer goods companies there is another C – the consumer which also needs to be considered. They are ultimately the ones buying your product and the customer is just a noisy person in between (with some requirements) that provides access to the consumer (or shopper).*

Storytelling

Being able to tell a story is becoming an increasingly popular topic in the finance business partnering space. As finance people we are objective in nature, meritocratic, and fact-based individuals. Stories are for the creative people and have no place in a world of accountability and performance. "Stories" sound like things people make up when they don't have the facts or are underperforming. Why tell stories when we have the facts? This is the way most of us approach this topic.

But that isn't storytelling. Storytelling is the ability to take pieces of information and join them together in a cohesive and compelling manner that either influences or entertains the audience. Now entertaining people may be great for the silver screen, but in the business world influencing the audience will suffice.

But how do we do this? What can we look to, to help us be able to tell better stories about the information we have at our disposal and provide some insight.

Greek philosophy may not be the space a lot of people would turn to for a storytelling framework but the works of Aristotle in his discussion of *Modes of Persuasion*[1] is a great structure and framework to guide a finance person into storytelling. It helps distinguish the pieces we are good at and the pieces that we need to consciously work on.

Modes of Persuasion looks at three dimensions of storytelling which will determine the success of what you are talking about. They are Ethos, Pathos and Logos.

Ethos; this talks to the credibility of the person telling the story. It is the ability of the person telling the story to convince the

1. See Aristotle (1991) *The Art of Rhetoric* (London: Penguin Classics)

audience that they have the authority or are qualified to speak on the topic. Without this people may not be engaged with what you have to say. This is fairly simple and straightforward for a finance person talking numbers in an organisation. However, in business partnering you may often be speaking about areas not of your area of expertise. In order to combat this, you can be introduced by the other functions (supporting your credibility), master the other function's "language" by understanding the terms they use, or by using some reference that gives gravitas to the fact you know what you are talking about. Sometimes referencing past roles or jobs can assist but be careful with the audience and how often you do this. It can become tiring hearing stories about what you did or what happened when you worked at x.

Ethos is often a given in presenting information and telling stories for finance staff. You have been asked to do it because you are the expert.

Pathos; this is the ability to use emotion to tell your story and is most effective when that emotion aligns to the audience. Telling a humorous story nobody laughs at because you are dealing with a sensitive issue is a sure fire way to ruin your Pathos. Every good storyteller has this in spades. They are able to identify the relevant emotion required for the story and bring that out in a way that the audience also feels that emotion. Sales and marketing do this very well. A great example is the "Deal on Today Only" emotion which forces you into a fear of missing out, thus forcing you to buy. Attempting to bring positive emotion to something when all of the facts and figures indicate a problem. Solutions attached to problems will fix this as will the excitement displayed in what the solution could be. Another way of bringing out the emotion is to use analogies, metaphors or similes. Taking a situation and comparing it to something the audience can relate to (such as the goalkeeper and pilot stories in "Understanding") is a way in which you can do this. Being specific and personal about a situation will also help to bring emotion – if something happened to you and you are able to convey those feelings by being deeply descriptive and specific you will be able to deliver on your Pathos.

Finance people have the most difficulty with this dimension as we are a fact-based function and objective by nature. We find it difficult to work in the subjective and potentially manipulate facts with emotion.

Logos; this is the ability to bring facts to support your story. This helps with the Ethos of a story as facts will help to support your credibility that you know what you are talking about. This is a strength of finance due to our objectivity and use of financial data to support a story. Every presentation we do will be supported by some form of table, graph, fact or data. The key is to ensure that fact or data is not misrepresented. As mentioned in the "Quality" section, if your left hand circles are not working well, and you go to present information that is of poor quality your Logos will be impacted.

Finance staff should find Logos the easiest dimension to work with. As opposed to sales who may use only a small part of the whole facts to support their story.

With those three dimensions in mind it is also worth remembering the place you choose to tell your story. This can have an impact on the cut through of what you are discussing. When I say place, it could be time of the day, location of office, audience's preparation to receive the information, etc. Attempting to tell a bad news story about a business issue at 3 pm on a Friday afternoon, dressed in corporate casual with a beer, when the executive team have been in a meeting for two hours previously celebrating something successful, is probably not going to deliver on the correct Pathos despite all of your best efforts.

As difficult and challenging as storytelling can be for a finance person, if you are able to understand the above three dimensions and elements you should be able to draw on enough information to be compelling. Facts and figures (Logos) shouldn't be a problem. You are often asked for your opinion when telling a story so that shouldn't be an issue (Ethos). However, Pathos (emotional connection to the audience) will always require work to bring the numbers and the finances, what some other functions may consider boring, to life.

Presenting Insight

The final aspect of providing Insight is to be able to present it in a compelling and persuasive manner to your business partners. By following the above, you will have collected information, thought about it from many aspects, made a judgment on what's known and what's assumption based, and you have worked out a good story that has some "Pathos".

Now it is time to present it. This in itself is an art and more and more importantly data visualisation skills are required.

The following is a list of methods and techniques to assist in bringing data alive in a presentation.

Headings are the story – when preparing your presentation, you are more than likely going to be using something like PowerPoint. As you work through the pages ensure that the headings to the pages tell the story. Standing alone with nothing else on the page the heading should be able to tell the story of your message. The data beneath it is the mechanism to bring "Pathos" and "Logos" to the story.

Analogies/metaphors – throughout this book there has been significant use of metaphors and analogies. Taking what you are talking about and turning it into something that is relevant or comparable for the audience. The goalkeeper and pilot metaphor for business partner is an example of this. By doing this you are simplifying the material for the audience and making it easier for them to relate to.

Anecdotes – stories and short fables about the topic you are talking about will assist in "Pathos" and connection with your audience. It helps you build rapport and connection. This comes with a warning to ensure any anecdote has some form of relevance to what you are talking about in the presentation.

Rule of Three – try to keep the number of things you are talking about to a maximum of three. Any more and the audience may lose the ability to understand what's important. Any less and you may lack depth and breadth in what you are talking about. For most business partnering problems and issues there is always more than one variable and complexity but going into each and every one can confuse people. Keeping it to a maximum of three will force you to focus, but it will also allow you to stay at a high level and go deeper if asked a question that requires some breadth.

Following on from the above techniques and methods the following are tools you can use to help with this as well:

Basic Graphs – line graphs and column graphs are the simplest and most basic form of data visualisation. Two lines or two bars are very impactful. They show something happening in comparison to something else at a very basic level and help focus attention. Too many lines and bars and you risk confusion.

Tables – personally I am not a big fan of tables, so I attempt to keep the use of them to a minimum. I recommend using them only when you need to show an entire and complete data set. If you wish to hone in on something a table is not recommended as there is too many distractions of other things that will cause discussion and if you do not include the entire data questions can be asked.

Heat Maps – in order to combat the above problem of tables, a heat map can be used. This will assist in focusing people's minds to the good or bad of the tables and areas that need focus as the heat moves in relation to the rest of the data. Everything becomes relative.

Waterfalls or Flying Bricks – the utilisation of waterfalls is great if you are attempting to show data moving from one place to another. Actuals to budget. This year to last year. The builds and declines are clearly shown and again in relation to each other, so focus can be provided. They can be tricky to format when moving data around so ensure the colours and the "bricks" line up and formatting is correct.

Bubble Charts – bubbles charts are a three-dimensional view of data, with a y and an x axis, plus size defined by the size of the bubble. It very quickly allows you to see what is big (important) and what is small (less important) as well as its positioning on two axes relative to others.

There are many ways of taking information and providing it in a manner that helps to provide context. The above is not an exhaustive list, but they are some of the most common and can be easily done in an accountant's favourite tool; Excel.

It is now time to pause, reflect and congratulate yourself. You are ensuring the quality of information you are using is there, you understand your organisation and you are starting to provide insight rather than information. If done well you will have built your credibility to a place where you are being asked to get involved in business critical issues, your opinion is valued, you will probably be busy and most importantly you can start to Influence the organisation you are in.

Section C

Influencing an Organisation

E is for Ethos & Mindset

In order to become a strong finance business partner there is a certain mindset that needs to be applied. An Ethos. Guiding principles. Concepts that define the way we think about the world and the approach and style we take into the dealings we have with our business partners.

The profession of accounting and finance that we have been brought up on has a similar structure and framework. Integrity, Objectivity, Competence and Due Care, etc. are all ingrained into us in our early studies. It is important we do not let these go as we work with other non-finance functions.

However, we need to blend this with other concepts and mindsets in order to be more effective with other functions. They do not speak our language, they do not understand why we must play by certain rules that they are not aware of and they do not understand we are trying to help rather than be a roadblock. The following concepts are there to assist in the way you need to think and apply an Ethos to your style as a finance business partners.

These concepts are the fundamental concepts and mindsets, or

Ethos, a finance business partner needs to apply to be effective:

- Getting to "Yes"
- Speak Their Language
- Keep Things Simple
- Avoid Emails
- Appetite to Understand
- "It Depends"

Getting to Yes

Getting to Yes is the first principle of the mindset required to be a strong finance business partner with other functions. Your job is to unlock and enable, not control and govern. You are the key to improving the business, not a roadblock preventing things from happening. You don't want to be known as the "sales prevention department".

Back in 2008, a new president of the United States of America, Barrack Obama gave his inauguration speech. The focus of his speech was captured in three short words:

"Yes, we can."

So simple, even Bob the Builder uses it – or did Obama borrow it from him? Jim Carrey made a movie about it called *Yes Man* where he decided to say "Yes" to everything.

As a Finance Business Partner, the concept of saying "Yes" to initiatives that are brought across your desk is a challenging one. We spend five or six years studying a framework of accounting standards, tax laws and quantitative analysis that is designed for answers that are either correct, or not correct, based on facts.

Yes or No, black or white.

We sit exams that encourage this by allocating marks for right and wrong answers. We often begin our careers as auditors, or Financial Accountants and advance to Financial Controller positions. These are often compliant in nature, have a high process function and are one of a "watchdog". We are regimentally trained there is a correct way of doing things and an incorrect way of doing things.

Our environment by its nature is one of two ends of a spectrum, with very little grey in the middle.

Unfortunately, the move into a business partner role, or a commercial role, requires a very different way of thinking to be effective with our non-finance business partners. Commercial roles are heavily focused on the top end of the P&L in areas such as sales, pricing, optimisation, investment, etc. A lot of this analysis and the initiatives we are asked to provide guidance on can have so many more qualitative factors surrounding them that far outweigh the quantitative. Market share, pet projects, new segments, costs of doing business, short-term tactical targets, increased costs that unlock opportunities, etc. Concepts that, on the surface and with a long term lens may not look like the best idea financially but need to be implemented to ensure the short term sustainability of a business and momentum is maintained.

Because of this our business partners in sales, marketing, operations need us to find a way to say "Yes", not "No". To continue moving forward and create momentum. We need to spend more time thinking of initiatives as "Good" and "Bad" ideas, rather than "Yes" or "No", and then how do we get these ideas to a "Yes".

So how do we do this? Three things that can help are:

Think "not yet" instead of "No"

When confronted with something that looks like a Bad Idea and probably a "No", ask yourself the question "What needs to happen to make this a Yes?" In its current form the initiative may not work but with a few tweaks and risk mitigation you may be able to get there. At the very least further diligence will be done to ensure the "No" is understood by your business partners who may have naively thought it was a no-brainer "Yes".

Measure and respond with pace

If something feels like it may be in the "bad idea" space, but has a lot of qualitative reasons for proceeding, it is wise to put in place strong tracking and measurement indicators. These should be reviewed regularly so that anything that you thought was a risk is identified early. Following on from that, alterations can be made so that the chance of success is improved. Remember execution is never linear. It is like tacking a yacht upwind. Rather than a straight line, you sometimes need to go left, right and around to get to the desired result.

Share decision making and insight

Involving other departments for their perspective will help identify opportunities and issues that you never thought of. Two heads are better than one and the collective is always worth more than the sum of the parts. Other departments have great insight on their areas of expertise and as a finance trained person you may never be aware of these. At the very least you may learn something new, and that can never be a bad thing.

The commercial world is complex. It requires a style of thinking that is not linear. A style that says, “In its current form I am not convinced, but if we do x, we can get there.”

Next time you are confronted with a piece of work that feels like an immediate “No” based on your financial training and discipline, be sure to take a step back. Think how we can make this better, and what am I not thinking of that may be qualitative.

Getting to Yes is what all organisations want from their commercial teams, and your unique skillset should be used to help the business say, “Yes we can.”

Speak Their Language

The second principle of strong finance business partnering is the ability to Speak Their Language. In other words, being able to communicate in the language of the function you are partnering and being able to understand their world completely.

Back in 2004 I spent a large portion of time overseas travelling around France. I would often find when talking to a "local" the first question I would ask was:

"Do you speak English?"

Most times, the response I got was a short, sharp "No!" – coupled with thoughts of how dare you request such a thing?

At other times, when I was conscious of where I was, I would try *"Parlez vous Anglais?"*

More often than not, the response to this was "Mmmm, a little," and perhaps a gesture that they would be happy to help me because I had made an effort to ***speak their language.***

Spending more time in the country I found myself picking up more phrases and words of the language, and the more I learned and spoke of their language, the more I understood and became more effective with the locals.

Being a Finance Business Partner to non-finance people is just like this. Sales, Marketing, Supply Chain, IT... they all speak their own language, and if you are not attuned to it, you will not be as effective as you need to be. And if you are not effective, you are going to find it difficult to "live in their country".

You also need to be able to understand the world from their point of view. Accounting Standards, Debits and Credits and even the art of arithmetic are all things we as accountants find familiar, and sometimes easy. It doesn't mean marketing does, it doesn't mean sales does.

They couldn't care less that a new lease standard is going to be introduced in a few years' time. They couldn't care that your balance sheet is going to change significantly. They probably don't even know what a Balance Sheet is (seriously they probably don't!). And nor should they, that is Finance's job.

Sales and Marketing are interested in things that are going to improve the top line. How can we sell more, grow customers, realise better prices, develop new segments, etc. That is what you need to be talking to them about. They have lots of ideas and experience, get beside them and know what they know. Go to a customer meeting, talk to your businesses target market, and learn to ***speak their language.***

IT want to talk to you about "your project", and Business Intelligence environments and their new whizz bang toy they have found. They want to scope everything and work with certainty. They are very introverted and generally avoid conflict. They don't understand the difference between capex and opex and the accounting standards that govern it. In their mind, they can capitalise anything and defer it to when they want to expense it. You need to find a way to translate your knowledge of estimate based accounting standards into something that makes sense for them. You need to ***speak their language.***

Supply chain and Operations are great at building efficiencies and cost improvement and lean processes. They are constantly under pressure to reduce costs. So, help them with this. What drives their costs, what is variable, what is fixed? What costs reduce quality and what costs increase quality. Sometimes investing some money can reduce things by a larger amount in other areas. Use the extensive business knowledge you have developed through your professional training to help them improve things that they haven't even thought of. They speak in a language that is often very direct and forthright. So, ***speak their language.***

As a Finance Business Partner, you have a unique position in an organisation to interpret some complex rules and regulations and access to a lot of information others don't see or cannot understand. But if this is not what helps your partner, you will never do yourself justice as a leader in an organisation. And you certainly won't be adding any value. So, spend time with your business partners, learn their function and above all learn to ***speak their language.***

Keep Things Simple

Leading on from speaking their language is the third principle of finance business partnering – ***"Keep Things Simple."***

Let's be very clear straight away. I will avoid reference to the KISS principle – ***Keep It Simple Stupid***. Insulting people is not a foundation for being a great Finance Business Partner. And I also do not intend to capture my thoughts in four words when I can do it in three and capture the same message without the insults. Instead, let's go with... Keep Things Simple.

As a finance business partner, we are often confronted with complex business problems, mountains of data, multiple reference points, various stakeholders, dozens of variables all requiring us to look through things from different lenses before coming to a conclusion/recommendation. We are neck deep in the detail for a lot of this work. And as meritocratic and righteous individuals, we believe that we need to disclose this knowledge in order to prove to people that we know what we are talking about.

Unfortunately, it works the other way in a commercial role within an organisation. Senior executives are under an enormous amount of time pressure. They don't need to know the detail. They know that you are all over it by the nature of the person and role you play. You don't need to prove it to them. What you need to do is distil the information down into a manageable form and communicate it with simplicity. ***Keep Things Simple.***

Albert Einstein made numerous references to this:

- "If you can't explain it simply, you don't understand it well enough."

- "Make everything as simple as possible, but not simpler."

- "If you can't explain it to a six-year-old, you don't understand it yourself."

Arguably one of the smartest men the planet has seen, working in one of the most complex areas of expertise, encouraging us all to ***Keep Things Simple***. I would suggest it's great advice.

So, as a Finance Business Partner, working in a world of so much information and opinions how do we ***Keep Things Simple.*** The following three concepts should assist

The Rule of 3; We briefly touched on this in the "Presenting Insight" section. Try to keep any discussion, presentation or meeting narrowed down to three key elements. The human brain cannot process much more than that. You risk losing people with what is important and what is not.

I learnt this on the drive to one of my first ever customer meetings when my sales business partner gave me a piece of advice. At the time it seemed so trivial and simple. When I asked him what the plan for the meeting was he told me, "I go into all of my meetings thinking about three things only."

Great I thought seems simple enough. "What are the three things?" I asked thinking I had unlocked the key to success. Give me the specific details now please.

His response was "It doesn't matter what they are, as long as there is no more than three."

This advice has stayed with me my whole career and is great advice for any finance business partner trying to solve complex business problems. Keeping your thoughts to three things helps you to ***"Keep Things Simple".***

Whether it is presenting in front of your executive team, discussions with staff members, management meetings, etc., by sticking to only three things that you want to discuss you force yourself to be more succinct. You force yourself to think more clearly and you force yourself to distil the multitude of information you have encountered along the way into easy to digest chunks and funnel down to what is really important.

Sticking to three things when there may be six or seven relevant items also leaves you with places to go if the conversation goes that way. If you show all of your cards and all of your information you will be less likely to have any place to go when questions come up. "Oh, have you thought about this?" If you have only spoken about the three most important things your likely response will be "Yes". If you have already disclosed everything you will be left exposed.

It will also make you appear more intelligent. Nothing is more of a reputation-killer than saying something is "complicated". What you are really saying is that you do not understand it well enough to be able to communicate it properly.

Use graphical representations; as human beings we are visual people. We like to see things in addition to hearing about it. We want to understand context and the "so what", and a graphical representation can do this very effectively.

Try to ensure your graphical representations are not overly complicated. As we discussed in the "Presenting Insight" section, if you can get them down to a line or bar graph that has only two to three lines, the cut through will be significant. Use greens and reds to identify "good" and "bad" and ensure your scales are relevant.

Never talk technical finance; nothing is more complicated to a non-finance person than a discussion about technical finance information. Accounting Standards, Tax Laws, Debits/Credits, etc. are a technical area you are employed to understand. Non-finance people do not want to know. Talking to someone about the new lease accounting standard that is about to be introduced, and the impacts on balance sheets of this change is a sure way to confuse a non-finance person. They don't know the accounting behind a lease, or the impact on a balance sheet of the change. As mentioned in "Speak Their Language" most of them don't even know what a balance sheet is. So, break it down to the impact it will have on them and the reasons it is important – for them, not for you. And avoid technical terms.

Keeping things simple is easier said than done. However, to avoid disengaging non finance business partners it is critical.

Keep Things Simple and remember:

"Complexity is your enemy. Any fool can make things complicated. It is hard to keep things simple" – Richard Branson

Avoid Emails

The fourth principle of strong finance business partnering is communication and we capture this in the statement "Avoid Emails".

The twenty-first century has allowed us to communicate in a number of effective and innovative ways. Email, Skype, Twitter, Facebook, Instagram, hashtags – the list goes on and on in relation to forms of communication which are anything but the simple and most basic form of communication; conversation.

The 7% rule proposed by Dr Albert Mehrabian,[3] tells us that communication is 7% verbal, 38% tone of voice and 55% body

3. See Mehrabian, A. (1971) *Silent Messages* (California: Wadsworth)

language. So, in an age where we over indulge in forms of communication that have no ability to show body language or tone of voice, how can we expect to communicate properly? In addition to this, these twenty-first century forms of communication allow us "thinking time" to craft a valid response and lose the benefits of instincts and spontaneity that often flow from the art of conversation and help us to develop our radar as a good business person. Business is about people first and foremost and if you are not able to function adequately with the tools of business (people) then you will be left behind as a finance business partner.

In business, and especially for finance staff wanting to become better business partners, there are distinct advantages to using conversation over emails. They include:

Issues are dealt with quickly

Having a conversation with someone means any questions or issues are dealt with immediately. For some reason we as humans believe that if we are sending an email, the person receiving it is reading it right then and there. They are not, and they may not read it until hours, days or even weeks later. And even if they do they don't have an obligation to respond immediately. They can choose whether to respond or to file it away in the "To Do" folder (or worse the Trash folder). Even if they do respond immediately, a two minute conversation can be an afternoons worth of emails back and forth. The average person types at a speed of 40–50 words a minute, whereas we speak at an average of 150–160 words a minute. Having a conversation is three or four times quicker which means issues are discussed and dealt with immediately or a plan is devised to resolve.

Reduced chance of misinterpretation

Ever read an email from someone and thought "Wow what does that mean?" Unfortunately, we are unable to convey tone over email and unless we have a degree in English and communication so often our written language is misinterpreted against what we were really trying to say – Language is important. I repeat LANGUAGE IS IMPORTANT (and this is not me yelling it is me emphasising it). We can kid ourselves that building in capital letters, bold and underlines and even emojis can help convey tone but they can't. The other person is reading the text from the emotional state they are in and are not aware of the emotional state you are in when writing it.

Body Language and Tone is very, very important to build rapport and relationships with people. With words only being 7% of the meaning wouldn't it be wise to utilize the other 93% and have a conversation.

Talking builds relationships

Talking to someone helps to build rapport and relationships with them. Sight, touch, smell, and sounds are a basic human function and sense. By having a conversation with someone you are experiencing all of these which helps to build stronger relationships. Its why we shake hands with people when we meet or see them.

For finance staff who are often dealing with problems or ensuring things are done a certain way, having this rapport to fall back on makes your message easier to deliver, and easier to receive.

You don't need evidence

Often people, and especially finance staff, will default to email to keep track of things and have evidence that they asked someone to do something, or for something, or to show they have completed something. Our training ensures we are like that. If you are working as a business partner and your relationship has got to the point where you need to refer to email strings to provide evidence of something, then it's too late. Your relationship and ability to business partner them has failed.

Under no circumstance does a business partnering relationship work if one of the parties is trying to catch the other one out or unravel them. It needs to be developed on trust and alignment and no email string will provide that. Conversations and relationships will overcome any situation where you just forgot or deleted something. Remember you work in the same organisation as the other person. You are on the same team, this sort of approach should be left for customers, suppliers or other external parties who want to be combative.

What about teams in different geographies?

The obvious challenge to getting away from emails is when your team or your business partner are in a different location to you physically. They may be in another office or worse in another time zone on the other side of the world and you are limited with your ability to have a conversation.

Telephone will assist with this, it will at least move you from 7% communication to 45% (7% words plus 38% tone). Even better is the use of tools such as Skype and video conferencing. There is no reason in this day and age that they can't be utilised. Time differences may mean you need to plan that more, however the investment is well worth the effort especially if they are from a different culture or speak a different language. Using just words to communicate in that instance is a sure fire way to offend people inadvertently and potentially damage your relationship.

So, next time you feel like you need to have a conversation, put the keyboard away and go and have an actual conversation with the person.

If your email has more than two replies in it, that is a conversation, so go and have one.

Appetite to Understand

The fifth principle of strong Finance Business Partnering is having an "Appetite to Understand". This talks to having strong curiosity and having the correct questioning and listening skills to extract information from people. These skills are key to helping you understand things further.

Asking Questions

Q: Why did the chicken cross the road?

A: To get to the other side...

This answer so obvious and satisfactory that nobody ever really goes any further. I would encourage anyone wanting to become a better Finance Business Partner to develop their curiosity, by asking one more question: "Why?"

Why does the chicken want to get to the other side?

Why is the chicken even on the road in the first place?

The ability to have a ***curious mind*** and develop the skill of wanting to know and understand more, is critical for a Finance Business Partner. It helps build your knowledge and understanding of business critical issues. This in turn will build your credibility and place you in a position where you are relied upon when important decisions need to be made.

The answers to the second, third and sometimes fourth and fifth "why" is what helps unlock business problems and create momentum to move forward. If you have this skill and are able to apply it, you will add more value than the analytics provided from spreadsheet calculations.

So how do you develop curiosity?

The Five Whys[4] is a great framework to use if you really want to understand something and get to the source of an issue. How does it work? Simply ask "Why" five times next time you are confronted with something you do not understand or want to develop some further knowledge on. For example,

1. Why did the chicken cross the road – to get to the other side

4. See Knowledge Solutions (2009) *The Five Whys Technique* (Philippines: Asian Development Bank)

2. Why does the chicken want to get to the other side – because there is food there

3. Why is the chicken looking for food – because it is hungry

4. Why are they hungry – because they got through a hole in the fence, wandered off and haven't eaten

5. Why is there a hole in the fence – the farmer hasn't repaired it yet

So really, if the farmer repairs the hole in the fence, the chicken won't be on the other side of the road and we won't have a hungry chicken. OK, let's fix the fence please.

As you can see from this if we continued to answer the question with "To get to the other side" we would have missed the problem. We would have also been dealing with the same question every day, until the problem was fixed, which is no way to run an effective operation.

When do you use this technique and how do you use it?

Unfortunately asking someone "Why" five times in a discussion or forum is a quick way to becoming known as combative and difficult to deal with. Under this sort of questioning most people will retreat to "fight or flight" and will resort to deflection, avoidance, humour or even blame as they become threatened. If your partner wants to "fight" or "flight", every time they deal with you, it's hardly going to create a great professional relationship.

Think about how you feel when children play the "why game" with you. Why, Why, Why... its very frustrating and you often get to the point of saying "I don't know just leave me alone".

The best time to use it is when you sense people are being vague, don't know the answer, or you sense there is risk in something and you need to know some more information. If someone says "It's complicated" that should be your trigger to dig deeper and simplify it.

Use leading or open statements like "Tell me more," "Go on," "That sounds interesting," or "Great, can we explore that some more, so I understand?" Silence can be a great tool too. Often the other person will fill that silence with more information.

So next time you are confronted with what seems like a simple question and an even simpler answer Ask "Why?". Always try to understand things at a deeper layer but do it in a way that is not threatening. This will help build your own knowledge, but also help bring your skillsets as a finance person to more commercial situations, and help you become a better Finance Business Partner.

The art of listening

I often get asked the question by finance business partners how can I develop my curiosity? How do I become more curious?

The first part to understanding and curiosity is by asking questions, the other part is to listen carefully.

The art of listening is a lost art in the busy world we live in, but a critical skill for a Finance Business Partner. A skill that will help you solve many a business problem, and add value to the organisation you are in.

As a finance business partner one of the key skills required of the role is to:

- identify business problems,
- understand the context and factors surrounding them, and
- provide commercial solutions that can be executed to fix them.

Most Finance Business Partners have a great skill at the first one - identifying business problems. We are trained to view things from an objective standpoint and will often be confused when things are done in the organisation that make no sense financially. If I asked you to make a list of your organisations business problems right now you could roll off a long list, I am sure.

For a finance person it is likely most would be quantitative in nature or have a process aspect to them.

Unfortunately, a lot of finance business partners get lost in the second one - understanding the context and factors that have created these problems.

And without this skill, there is no chance of being able to perform the third - provide commercial solutions that can be executed to fix them.

What you will be left with is a theoretical solution which is unable to be executed within the context of the organisation you are in.

In order to break this and add value to your organisation you need to practice the art of listening. I'm not sure who said this or whether it is just a statement of fact but...

"God gave us two ears and one mouth, use them in proportion," or similarly...

"God gave us mouths that close, and ears that don't."

Put simply, turn off your mouth and turn on your ears. You are designed that way.

As a former senior finance executive who is now a consultant, this skill is key to anything I do. I must fully understand what the problem of my client is and am being asked to solve. I cannot jump to conclusions and I must be patient in order to land on what that is. This can take some time but without it I am unable to determine whether I can help you. Once I understand it though, the solution is often obvious. It saves me time and my clients money. I need to have an "Appetite to Understand".

Finance Business Partnering is the same. You must listen to what people are saying, from all angles, distil it, think about it, go back again with your thoughts and repeat. And then repeat again if necessary. Until the problem is articulated and simplified and until that Appetite to Understand is fulfilled.

So how do you do this – **by listening.**

Practice silence; if you do not speak others with opinions will fill that void. This can be gold as it provides more and more context. It doesn't need your input. If they continue to speak they may come to the correct conclusion themselves.

Make notes; document your conversations verbatim. Don't put them in your own words, write them down as they were said. This creates zero confusion if you need to recall them later and think about what was discussed. By writing you are also giving your colleagues a chance to talk which non finance people love, if they think you are listening.

24 Hour Rule; spend 24 hours distilling what you have been told. Your instinctual answer may be the correct one, but spend time thinking about it. You may have missed something that was lost in the excitement of being present in the discussion. For a finance person being accurate is just as important if not more than being quick.

And last but not least say "thank you" and smile. The art of manners and showing your teeth not only biologically makes you feel good, it makes the people around you feel good. It is a great way to end a conversation and at the very least makes the other person feel like they were being listened to and you are on top of things.

And your Appetite to Understand will hopefully be fulfilled.

"It Depends"

The sixth and final principle to strong Finance Business Partnering is the concept of "It Depends". This manifests itself in your ability to embrace and understand three things; Complexity, Ambiguity and Context. Understanding that the questions you will be asked and the information you are provided with will all be done with the aim of you providing an "answer" or a recommendation.

Your initial response to any question of this type should always be "It Depends" (or, what is the context?).

What price can I go to on this? Is this business case ok? Can you please approve this spend?

Well it depends. On many things. Most we don't know and most we can't control. It depends. And being comfortable saying that and then exploring it is critical.

Context can be achieved through questioning and listening as we discussed in "Appetite to Understand" however being comfortable working in the ambiguous and the complex can be challenging for a finance person who has spent their entire career in a black and white compliance world.

Be comfortable being uncomfortable

Complexity and Ambiguity are concepts that increase significantly once you start to play in a commercial role, start working with other functions, develop a strong understanding of your organisation and the environment it operates in. Why? Because you are dealing with a lot more information that is not perfect and you are dealing with a lot more creatures known as humans who all think differently and approach business issues from different angles.

“Being comfortable in the uncomfortable” is critical if you are not to lose your mind as a finance business partner. Interpretation and judgment becomes very important.

Consider the following email you have just received from the head of your operations department:

“I need some analysis done on our variable costs, if we don’t get these under control and heading in the right direction soon we are going to have to make some tough choices.”

Now if I was to read that as a logic-based finance person, my mind would suggest that this is not a request to do anything. It would indicate that there is most likely some work to be done but the specifics of the request will probably come later. But there is no clear direction, there is no context and there is certainly no direct reference to anything they are looking at or for.

Many finance people struggle with this. Where do you begin? What are they asking? Should I go and talk to them or wait for further instruction.

A good finance business partner will read this and start to formulate an approach immediately. This request has come from a place of tension or stress and some assistance is being requested. Exactly what that is, and the clarity behind it is not needed to start to pull together some information that may be able to assist.

Be comfortable with this.

Your answer won't be correct, and what you provide won't be the end of the request.

Be comfortable with this.

It may be a review that is short and easy to perform or a detailed deep dive. In the middle of an already busy schedule where you aren't getting to your "To Do list" already

Be comfortable with this.

This is the nature of finance business partnering roles. Complex requests, continually coming, no context, no timelines.

Be comfortable with this.

And remember the Ethos section on emails. If you think it requires a conversation, have a conversation.

Perfectionism

Another area that causes a lot of procrastination within finance business partners and finance teams is the tension between having perfect figures or being materially correct. This is drilled into us through our training.

Are these numbers good enough, or do I need to do some further checking and analysis?

Unfortunately, there is always a battle happening between one plus one equalling two, or one plus one equalling 1.9 and knowing when to move on or dig a little deeper.

For a finance individual the amount of time wasted or invested in this decision is critical.

Are you a person who likes to operate in the detail or do you prefer to see things at a high level?

Are you a perfectionist or is near enough good enough?

The former is a common interview question for finance people looking to get into Business Partner roles, the latter – well, I guess we would all like to think we are perfect.

Take this example. You have been given a very important piece of work to do that will have high impact on the organisation you work in. It's urgent. And there is pressure to ensure it is accurate and reliable.

Which end of the spectrum do you operate at? The person who goes away and spends a significant amount of time looking into every detail and attempting to come to an answer or recommendation that is perfect. Or the person who collects the basic information known, makes a couple of high-level assumptions and produces something that sort of feels right (and was potentially done on the back of an envelope).

As a finance business partner this situation and decision is at the forefront of most things we do. And as finance people it is drilled into us from an early stage in our career to be thorough and accurate. Cross-referencing every part of the file to another part of the file to ensure it stands up in court is common practice for someone who chose to start their career in audit. Keeping timesheets for every six minutes we spend on a client. Everything we do early in our careers and through our formative training in the industry, conditions us for the detailed approach.

Unfortunately, in the pressurised environment of a commercial organisation where decisions are required quickly and accurately because customers can be unreasonable, being thorough and detailed needs another solution. Being perfect can mean missing opportunities.

So, what is the preference for a finance person, detailed or high level. Should we go to Perfecttown, where detail rules and nothing ever gets completed?

My advice is to not see these things as mutually exclusive (and an "or" question) but more a polarity to high performance. And this polarity is dependent on your knowledge or experience in something. If you know little about something, this lack of knowledge forces you to spend time to gain an understanding. Once you have gained that understanding, the law of diminishing returns kicks in where any further time spent acquiring knowledge does not actually add any value and you need to move into a high-level approach to operate at a high performance.

The following model helps to demonstrate this with each quadrant requiring a different approach:

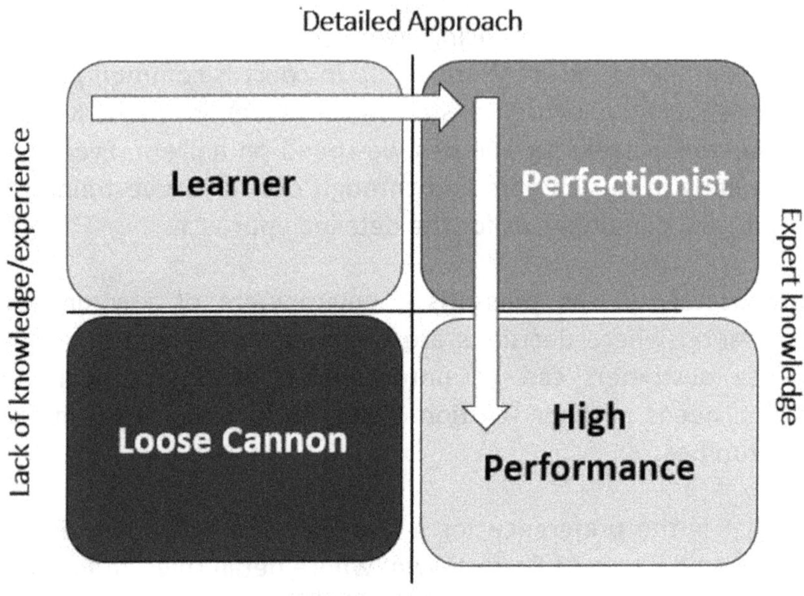

Figure 6: Perfectionism

Loose Cannon; this quadrant is for people who have very little knowledge in a subject and no interest in learning the detail. Their depth of knowledge is low, and they would rather just know the headlines. They often like to wing it (and use fancy words to portray knowledge) or employ people below them who will look into the detail. Asking this person for advice is considered very risky as it will not come from a place of great depth or it will have been garnered through their staff and may miss important details or be filtered inappropriately. These people often make mistakes and lose credibility very quickly within an organisation (and if they are in management are very frustrating for the team below them). They will apply a high-level approach to most things and risk providing poor recommendations.

Learner; a learner is also someone who has little knowledge or experience of something but is keen to get an understanding and is willing to spend the time to understand it. They will be very eager to gather information that helps them to learn more about something. This approach is often a very detailed approach as time is required to gather, understand and interpret what you have come across. For a finance individual this is often in the new stages of a role when you are determining the technical aspects of the role, who does what, how do I get information out of the system, or simply how does this spreadsheet work. This is a critical area for any finance individual wanting to be a successful business partner to other functions as you need to be prepared to understand their world.

Perfectionist; this is a person who has great knowledge or experience in something but is unable to move away from the detail. A giveaway if you are in this position is that you seem to have a lot of work mounting up, are more than likely working very long hours and nobody can understand why. You are risk-averse to giving recommendations and insight despite being in a position where you should have a great depth of knowledge on something and when asked for advice the default response is "It's complicated." A perfectionist spends too much time in the detail when a high-level approach is required and their depth of understanding on something warrants a simpler approach. If you find yourself in this quadrant you either need to go back to the learning quadrant and spend time in the detail to understand it better in order to simplify it, or quickly recognise you are spending too much time in the detail, trust your knowledge and move into the high performance quadrant.

High Performance; this quadrant is the equivalent of mastery and if you have taking the journey from top left to bottom right you will have acquired enough knowledge on something to allow you to operate at a higher, less detailed level. You will have plenty of envelopes in your office with just the back of them written on. You know your information well, you also know where to go to get information you aren't able to recall instantly. You can identify when something isn't quite right and requires more depth of understanding. In short you have spent time understanding something at the required depth to be able to operate at a high level.

Based on this framework it is clear to see that the answer to the question of "Are you a detailed person or a high level operator?" is: "It depends". And it will depend on your depth of knowledge on something. Try to do it short hand with no knowledge and you risk your credibility (loose cannon). Likewise, being too detailed when your knowledge suggests a quicker response (perfectionism) will also damage your credibility, not to mention your available time. Instead get involved in something, spend the time to learn it and understand it well enough so that you can operate at a high level when asked for your advice on things.

Please remember the following two quotes:

"The enemy of good is perfection" – Voltaire
and
"If you can't explain it simply, you don't understand it well enough" – Albert Einstein

Your Ethos and your mindset towards being a Finance Business Partner is critical in your success. Your Ethos wraps itself around every other part of the QUIET framework to Finance Business Partnering for a reason as each and every one of the six principles finds its way into the other areas on a regular basis. If you can align to the principles you will have a much stronger mindset and approach that will allow you to have stronger influence with your teams, your peers and your stakeholders.

T is for Trust

The final element that is critical to the success of a Finance Business Partner is their ability to develop trust among the network of people they work with within the organisation. By having your business partners trust you, you will be in a position to Influence them more effectively.

By following the QUIET framework to date, you will have produced good Quality information, you will Understand with breadth and depth how the organisation operates, and you will be producing vast amounts of Insight that ensures your credibility. You will also be operating with an Ethos or Mindset that is helping you behave in a certain way that you can start to Influence others, but we need to be more targeted with that to develop trust.

Without Trust, Influence is not going to be able to be accomplished.

As has been mentioned several times throughout this book, 42% of non-finance leaders are looking for accuracy from their finance team. In other words, they want to trust you and the information you provide them. They know we have access to large amounts of information, spanning the entire organisation. They are looking for you to distil this and provide relevant and reliable information for decision making.

Unfortunately, developing this trust requires different behaviours depending on who you are dealing with in an organisation. What works well for you and the individuals in your direct finance team, will be different to working with your peers in other departments, which will then be different from what works well with your boss, your boss's boss and your boss's peers.

Certain behaviours work well with some, and not so much with others. Your ability to flex your style and behaviours in different environments is critical to maintaining this trust and ensuring you can continue to influence.

Before we step into the model developed for this book it is important to step back and reflect on a separate model that is very relevant when attempting to develop trust. The Trust Equation or the Trust Quotient as defined by Charles H Green in his series *The Trusted Advisor*[5] is the most relevant source. In his works he found the formula for increasing trust with people was defined as:

(Credibility + Reliability + Intimacy) / Self-orientation

In other words, if you increase your Credibility, or you increase your Reliability, or you increase your Intimacy with others (or a mixture of both) then their trust in you will also increase. Conversely if you increase your Self-orientation or interest in your own needs, then their trust in you will decrease (and vice versa).

With this source of authority in mind let's examine the seven behaviours required of a finance business partner in order to be

5. See Green, Charles H., Maister, D. and Galford, Robert M. (2000) *The Trusted Advisor* (New York: Touchstone)

successful with the range of people and functions you will need to work within an organisation.

The "A" Frame

Through the research done in the development of this book we discovered that finance business partners will generally work with three types of individuals. These are the people we need to influence:

- The finance team they lead (Leading Finance teams)
- The non-finance staff they work with (Working Cross-Functionally)
- The senior staff above you in finance and other departments (Managing Stakeholders)

We also discovered in the research that across this spectrum of individuals there were seven key behaviours or characteristics that stood out as important when trying to influence these individuals. Conveniently we have bundled these behaviours into words that start with "A":

- Authenticity
- Availability
- Awareness
- Accountability

- Agility
- Alignment
- Assurity

From the three layers of individuals finance business partners work with, and the seven behaviours that are required to build trust and influence with them, we developed the . . .

3 x 7 "A" Frame . . .

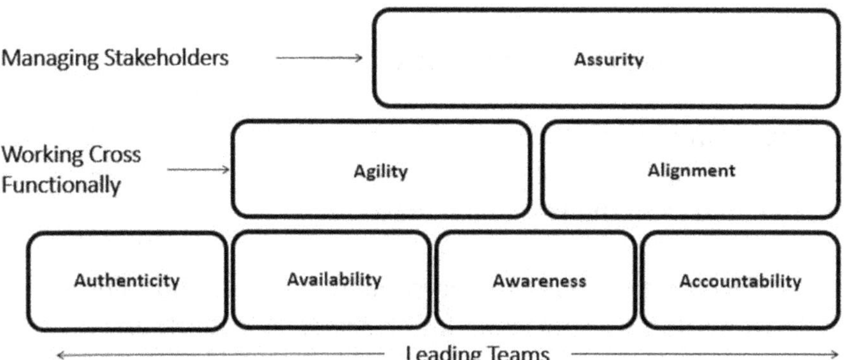

Figure 7: The "A" Frame

This framework forms the basis of the behaviours required to be a successful finance business partner. If you are able to master these behaviours and apply them in your working interactions with the relevant staff, you will be well on your way to developing the trust required to influence them and the organisation. In some form or another they will increase your Credibility, Reliability and Intimacy, and help to reduce your Self-orientation.

Leading Finance Teams

Building Trust within your direct Finance team is the first element of Trust that a Finance Business Partners needs to develop. Following on the importance of the Quality and Understanding sections, it will often be your team that is producing or providing this work. They will be performing month ends, forecasts, budgets, they will be working in the business and providing information and insight for you to take to the rest of the organisation. If you did not have your team around you, you would be far too busy to deal with all of the requirements of the role of a Finance Business Partner. You need a team of people to assist you either under your direct or indirect control and influence.

So, your team has to have trust in you and you have to have trust in them to ensure you can operate effectively.

During the research of what made a successful finance leader, four key behaviours came out in all of the answers. These answers were triangulated from the two main questions:

- "What behaviours and personality traits do you think are important to your team in their finance leader", and
- "What behaviours and personality traits do you expect of your own finance leader".

The four key behaviours that came out were Authenticity, Availability, Awareness and Accountability

Authenticity

Authenticity was highlighted as a critical behavioural component of leading effective finance teams. It over indexed versus other functional teams. 41% of Leaders said they think their team expects this of them and 49% of team members said they expect this of their leader.

Descriptive words used to display this included being transparent, genuine, caring, honest and empathetic. Having integrity, trust and belief in others. Displaying positivity, vulnerability, connection and the ability to listen.

Authenticity specifically manifests itself in finance people due to the nature of our training and conditioning in our function. Words like integrity, due care, competence, etc. are all instilled into us from the relevant professional accounting bodies. They are drilled into us in our profession and it makes us somewhat meritocratic in nature on a daily basis. We strive for what is right and what is fair and when we don't see it we disengage quickly. More so than other functions. If we don't believe you and think that you are hiding something and not being genuine it fights against our very nature to trust you. This is more so in finance individuals than other functions due to our conditioning in our profession.

Signs you are strong in this space is that people gravitate to you. They want to share their stories and their experiences with you. They reach out to you for your opinion. You will see your team members coming to you and displaying this. In a way they seek your approval and respect you. You feel like there is no agenda when you are around someone with strong authenticity, and they will often seek and provide feedback on just about anything.

Unfortunately, there is a downside to having a strong Authenticity read. You tend to over-index in your emotions and wear your heart on your sleeve. You disclose too much information at times and can over play your authenticity to a point where the trust balance goes the other way because you are behaving in line with your own self orientation (the denominator of the trust equation). People are unsure as to what to expect from you, someone who is composed or someone who just wants to be themselves all of the time. For anyone who enjoys a sport analogy, you could be the best most exciting player in the football team, but it doesn't necessarily make you captain. This may be because you are not aligned to the values of the larger group.

The balance between being very authentic to attract the following and belief you need your team to have in you, needs constant monitoring with the information and emotions you choose to display. Too authentic, can destroy trust. Not authentic, can destroy trust. There is a balance.

Accountability

Accountability is all about getting things done. 34% of leaders said they think their team expects this of them whereas surprisingly only 21% said they expected this of their manager. This would imply that it is even more important for you to accomplish tasks if you are part of the team rather than leading them team.

Descriptive words used to display this included being responsible, conscientious, competent, and intelligent (understanding finance strongly). Providing reliability, as well as being extremely motivated, results driven and passionate.

Accountability often finds itself into finance people by the nature of the work we do. Very task and deadline driven means we must complete things to a high level to avoid coming back and revisiting them. If we make a mistake it stands out (see Understanding your Role). Accordingly getting things done, on time and error-free is not uncommon. We are conditioned to be accountable and responsible.

Signs you are strong in this space are that you regularly meet deadlines accurately and on time, and you attract work and projects to yourself (because people know they will get the desired result). You are considered by most to be a subject matter expert in your area, and you have a kind of sick attraction to getting to work on Mondays as you don't want to let people down and want to be there in a time of crisis.

The downside to this is that you will probably have a work–life balance problem. As you enjoy what you do and have high levels of achievement, your desire to be successful at work can sometimes override a personal life. It can also manifest itself in an inability to read other people's priorities and what may be important to them. As you are so focused on your own world and achieving what you need you may become blind to others needs and lack the empathy to see this. Just because you love what you do and are regularly there solving problem and providing deliverables, doesn't mean everyone else is on the same page.

For Finance team members they expect some form of expertise in their manager to successfully lead them. It can be a complex discipline, they expect them to know their trade and they expect a commitment to the cause from their leader. They expect you to be Accountable.

Availability

The third dimension to Effectively Leading Finance teams is this concept of being Available to them. You need to be "Around". Only 16% of Leaders said they thought their team considered this important but 24% of team members identified it as important. This tells us that as a leader you might not think it's important to be around for your team, but they expect it from you.

Descriptive words used to display this included being reachable, accessible and around when needed. But just being around is not enough, you need to be supportive and approachable, and get involved and collaborate with the team and develop and coach your team.

Availability is the one behaviour within a finance leader that is either over- or under-indexed. Finding the right equilibrium between enough but not too much is a significant challenge. What team members are really asking for here is development, and interest in their development. A manager that has strong readings of Availability, has a team trumps individual attitude and they see their role as the leader to drive this into their team.

My personal mindset, style and approach to this is that "It is my job as the leader to ensure that my team believes that I believe in them".

They also have strong resilience and coping mechanisms. People will regularly come to your desk or office with requests. Keeping your door closed, and shutting yourself off to them, not giving them your full attention when in your office are sure ways to indicate to people that you are there, but you are not really "Available".

Unfortunately, there is a downside to being too Available. You get nothing done. You can tend to work long hours as you have an unhealthy obsession to wanting to be there for people. This can come across as intruding and at its worst taking a micromanaging approach, as you want to be involved in every little detail and be across everything. This can do the opposite to what being Available intends in that your team sometimes just need to be left to develop and get on with their responsibilities with the trust and belief that they will be ok.

Being around to develop your team is critical to developing trust with them. If they don't think you believe in them, don't think you trust them, don't provide them with opportunities and are not there to guide them, you cannot expect them to repay the faith and trust you.

Awareness

The final behaviour required to Effectively Leading Finance teams is Awareness. This directly relates to your Emotional Intelligence and your ability to have a strong radar for the organisation and the people within it. Some 9% percent of leaders said they thought their team considered this important and only 6% of team members identified it as important in their leader.

Descriptive words used to display this included having empathy, understanding the nuances of humans and people, having a strong radar and being very perceptive and knowing when to "push the accelerator" and when to "apply the brakes". It also came through being able to communicate effectively.

There are obvious strengths and plus sides to having strong awareness. You can wear different hats in different situations, you are comfortable being uncomfortable and ambiguity and complexity do not phase you. You appreciate the qualitative as well as the quantitative, and you understand there is more to the work and business problems than the task itself.

Is there any downside to having strong awareness? If you let it overtake your thoughts, then yes. Nothing will get done as you become too preoccupied with the human side of things or paralysis by analysis. You can get too involved in office politics or involved in too many things meaning nothing takes your focus. Having a strong radar means you pick up signals others don't, and this can occupy a lot of your mind that it doesn't for others.

Having strong awareness assists not only your ability to influence your team but how your team can utilise you in their workings within the organisation. If you are able to communicate this quality to your team they will be able to operate more effectively.

Now that we have gone through the Four Key Behaviours for Leading Effective Finance Teams it is important to understand their position in the 3 x 7 "A" Frame as shown in Figure 8.

All four sit at the bottom of the "A" frame, with Authenticity on the far outside left. Accountability and Awareness sit to the right of centre and Availability in the middle left. We will explain the importance of these position as we work through the other dimensions.

Working Cross-Functionally

We have previously spoken at length of the skills required to work with other functions within an organisation outside of finance. Being able to "Speak Their Language" and "Keep Things Simple" are both mindsets and principles to allow you to operate with people in other functions who do not naturally know or understand what you know and understand.

In addition to this there are certain qualities and behaviours that these other functions require from you in order to build trust with them. You will be working with them on a daily basis, so having a strong relationship, rapport and trust with each other will allow your dealings with them to be more effective. Remember nobody likes working with someone they find difficult and they are less likely to disclose all of the information they need to if they feel threatened all of the time. You need to be "QUIET".

Agility

The first behaviour required to work with people in other functions is being able to have Agility. You need to have the intellectual and emotional horsepower to be able to operate in many different environments and make finance easy for people to understand. 33% of non-finance leaders said this was important to them in their finance business partners.

Descriptive words used to display this included being flexible, approachable and adaptable. Being comfortable in the uncomfortable, but also bringing a level of composure and consistency to your work so that you can be depended on. You are dealing with a complex and difficult topic for a lot of people outside of finance and you need to be able to communicate in a flexible and basic manner and "dumb down" finance concepts.

Signs that you are strong in this area is that you are able to explain finance concepts, simply to non-finance people. Getting caught up in jargon, calculations and standards and laws is not effective when working with non-finance people. You also need to be able to prioritise and wear many different hats. Lots of things like projects or initiatives will be coming your way and you need a mechanism to manage this and determine where you invest your time. And you need to respond with speed. If you are working with sales, customers like an answer today, be prepared to set yourself up to deal with that. You are also required to clear problems and provide solutions for people, not roadblock things. You are an enabler and you need to get to "Get to Yes".

The biggest issue for finance business partners working in this space is their inability to get out of the black and white and being rattled by uncertainty and wanting to be perfect (stuck in the detail). Being stuck on what is right and what is wrong, being meritocratic and trying to get to a perfect answer are all inhibitors to working effectively with non-finance people. When you feel like you are stuck on something and are potentially a roadblock rather than an enabler ask yourself these two questions:

"Would you rather be right, or would you rather be effective?"

"What is the risk of me being wrong, and what is the impact if I am?"

If the answer to the second question is high, manage your stakeholders around the work required to get to "Get to Yes".

Being able to deal with the myriad of requests you have as a finance business partner, along with your ability to explain finance to non-finance people is another element of successful finance business partnering. We call this Agility and without it you will be stuck doing the transactional work.

Alignment

The second behaviour required to work with people in other functions is Alignment and being able to get onto the same page as them. The majority of the time you will be working on initiatives where you are coming from completely different functional perspectives. If you are unable to agree and align the chances of a successful trusting relationship between you will be diminished.

Descriptive words used to display this include understanding their perspective often developed through listening and spending time with them and being curious. They are also keen to have you challenge and discuss with them their thoughts in a respectful and supportive manner. Other non-finance functions want you to understand their area, marry it with your functional knowledge and navigate through any discrepancies.

Signs that you are strong in this area is that you are able speak the language of their function, understand their KPIs and motivations, and are able to hold a conversation as if you were part of their department. You are able to be an enabler for them rather than a roadblock and you are able to disagree with them, but you work through it amicably so that you are aligned.

Finance business partners who are unable to do this get stuck "policing" the other functions and not understanding their perspective or the world through the other functions context. This would normally force you into a space where you are over-involved in what they do and a roadblock or under involved in what they do and passive. This creates a tension where either party will be unhappy with the relationship and make it difficult to build strong trust within it. Accordingly getting alignment and on the same page is a key behaviour in order to be a strong finance business partner.

So, we have gone through the four behaviours required to lead an effective finance team and we have positioned them on the A Frame. Now it is time to layer in Agility and Alignment into it.

Alignment is on the right hand side of the middle layer as shown in Figure 8, with Agility on the left. The reasons for this become apparent when we discuss Managing Stakeholders.

You will also notice in Figure 9 that we have dropped off Authenticity as a key behaviour for working with non-finance individuals. Despite Authenticity being a key behaviour to manage and lead a finance team it wasn't highlighted in our research when working cross-functionally. My hypothesis is that this is because Authenticity has some form of Self-orientation to it, which if when referring to the Trust Quotient, would lead to a decrease in trust. The other functions are also neither here nor there as to whether you behave in a manner that is genuine and transparent and in accordance with your values. Accordingly, this behaviour drops off and leaves us with Accountability, Awareness, Availability, Agility and Alignment as the five key behaviours or working cross-functionally.

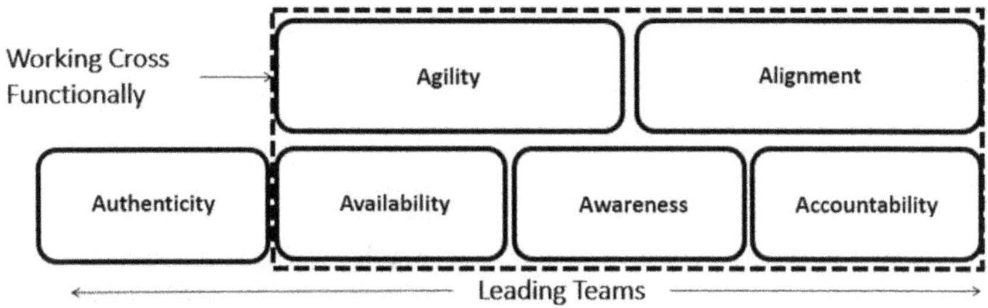

Figure 8: 5 Key behaviours for working cross functionally

Managing Stakeholders and your Reputation

The final constituent of the A Frame for a Finance Business Partner to build trust with is your stakeholders. Your boss, your boss's boss, and your boss's peers. These are the people who sit above you in an organisation and have a significant influence on your career within the organisation. Ironically, they are the ones that probably spend the least amount of time with you, have limited interactions at a deep level with you, and discuss you with each other on a regular basis to determine whether you will progress through an organisation. A comment here or there, your body language, presence and input in meetings are all things they observe, note and file away for a discussion at a later time. It is highly likely these discussions are focused on moments rather than days and is why continuous and conscious effort needs to be made every day to futureproof your prospects within the organisation.

One behaviour stands out above all others for a Finance Business Partners as important when dealing with the stakeholders above you. We have previously mentioned that 42% of all non-finance leaders expect Accuracy from their finance team. This Accuracy is required to build trust, credibility and faith in your ability to deal with the finances of the organisation. This manifests itself in a word we call Assurity.

Assurity

Descriptive words used to display this include the obvious one of accuracy. But also, confidence, trust, belief and knowledge. They want to know you are able to bring a balanced well-considered view (hence being QUIET), applying strong business and organisational acumen and where appropriate be able to provide solutions to problems and resolution.

Signs that you are strong in this area are first and foremost that your numbers are not in question. You are in the finance department so ensuring the discussion is on the insight from your numbers rather than whether they are correct is critical. Invest time in ensuring this occurs before any interaction with them.

You will also be sort out for your opinion and most likely be put in projects and tasks that are important to the organisation. You do not put your best players in the place on the field where there is no action. So, if you are being asked to work on things that are being spoken about a lot by your peers and stakeholders it's a sign they have confidence and Assurity in you. Most finance people with this behaviour will act as a conscience of the organisation and treat it like they are the owner.

On the opposite side if you aren't being asked to get involved in important projects, it is a strong sign the staff above you in an organisation have a question mark over you. Being too polarising can also be a problem. Some people want the "powers that be" above them talking about them at the boardroom table, or in talent reviews. On the flip side if they are spending too much time speaking about you, it signals they are not aligned and disagree and may find you polarising. This isn't a good thing and may lead to a lack of feedback for you.

Assurity – the one behaviour the people above you in an organisation want from a finance business partner and fits right atop the A Frame:

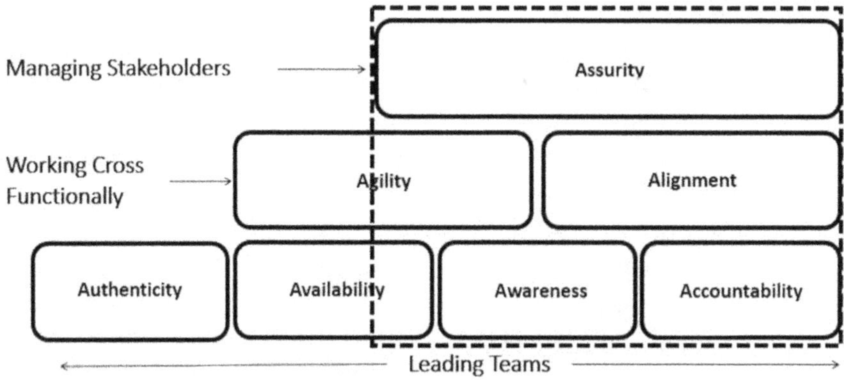

Figure 9: 4 Key behaviours for working stakeholders

You will notice in Figure 9 the distinction being made on Availability and Agility and the dotted line surrounding them is not quite complete. The reason for this is that although both are important when dealing with stakeholders above you, they can be flexed.

The people above you are very busy and understand you probably are too, so Availability drops down a little. I would not recommend not being there when they request work, but they do understand you are juggling several priorities as they are. Agility also drops down a little in importance as they are able to speak finance adequately. They could adequately hold a conversation around numbers or technical accounting if needed. So, the skill required for that Agility is less important than with your peers.

This leaves four remaining that are critical to working with your boss, your boss's boss and your boss' peers. Assurity, Accountability, Awareness and Alignment.

Building Trust with your business partners is a critical element to working effectively in an organisation. The Trust Equation as defined by Charles H Green in his works on the Trusted Advisor also talks to common elements noted above. You should have noticed a common element of the above behaviours falling into one or more of the above elements of the Trust Equation i.e. Assurity/Accountability and Credibility, Accountability/Availability/Alignment and Reliability, Awareness/Availability and Intimacy, etc., etc. And all of them (with potentially the exception of Authenticity) do not increase Self-orientation or Self-interest.

Putting QUIET to work

We have been through the 3 x 7 "A" Frame now and have highlighted the key behaviours that were sighted in our research when working as a finance business partner in an organisation. These also weave their way in and out of the works of Charles H Green in his Trusted Advisor works.

With your trust levels now high within your organisation you are ready to self-reflect on your journey to becoming a better finance business partner.

The quality of work you are producing is of a high standard. Your left hand circle work is being minimised and your right hand circle work is improving every day. This allows you to be seen as adding value in an organisation.

You have spent time in the organisation building your Organisational Acumen. Teaching and Learning from the people will hold you in good stead to be able to provide insight and add even further value. You are also able to speak the language of other functions and be able to translate technical finance in a way they understand, unlocking your effectiveness to them.

You are also able to bring all of the information and knowledge together into Insight. Telling stories effectively and bringing data to life in compelling presentations have assisted you to deliver that insight to your organisation.

And you have done it in a way that is true to the six principles of Finance Business Partners. Getting to Yes, Speak Their Language, Keep Things Simple, Avoid Emails, Appetite to Understand and "It Depends" should all be front and centre of your mind when working in the organisation. Enabling, getting involved, communication, curiosity, listening skills, asking questions, context, ambiguity, complexity and being comfortable being uncomfortable are all captured in these six principles.

The final step is then to take this and build trust with EVERYONE in the organisation. There are different ways to do this with different people, finance teams are different to cross functional teams. But you now have a 3 x 7 A Frame tool to help direct you in the behaviours that work in this space.

In addition to what has been discussed in this book there are a multitude of additional models and financial concepts that can fit nicely into the finance business partnering field. These are generally very specific in nature to each individual and organisation. I hope that the QUIET approach helps in identifying where you may see your issues either individually and organisationally, and if you need to go deeper on any of these topics my team would be more than happy to assist.

If you apply the QUIET approach to Finance Business Partnering in a consistent and regular manner, I have no doubt you will have moved your accounting career from "Compliance to Commercial" and become a Better Finance Business Partner.

About the Author

Andrew Jepson has quickly become one of Australia's leading presenters and authorities on finance business partnering. Through this passion he developed the "Compliance to Commercial" Development Program to assist emerging finance talent navigate their development as a business partner, and expand their influence in commercial and operational decisions.

With over 20 years of practical commercial Finance & Accounting experience Andrew has blended practical skills & knowledge with recent independent research, to help develop a framework for finance business partnering.

Andrew is available for inhouse training programs for finance teams looking to expand their influence in commercial organisations.

www.ingramcontent.com/pod-product-compliance
Lightning Source LLC
Chambersburg PA
CBHW062028200326
41519CB00017B/4970

* 9 7 8 0 6 4 8 3 4 2 3 0 4 *